CONFIRMATION

*The celebration of
maturity
in Christ*

CONFIRMATION
The celebration of maturity in Christ

Urban T. Holmes, III

A Crossroad Book
SEABURY PRESS · NEW YORK

The Seabury Press
815 Second Avenue
New York, N.Y. 10017

Library of Congress Cataloging in Publication Data

Holmes, Urban Tigner, 1930–
    Confirmation: the celebration of maturity in
Christ.

    1. Confirmation. I. Title.
BV815.H6   234'.162   75-15879
ISBN 0-8164-2589-2

For Mollie and Anne
"The beauteous seraph sister-band"

Contents

Preface

Bishop Paul Haynes in his first address before the convention of the Diocese of Southwest Florida made the observation that Christian initiation is the critical question of liturgical revision and that Confirmation lies at the heart of the question. This book is written in the spirit of this conviction to seek some greater understanding of the issue of Confirmation.

In a review of my book, *Young Children and the Eucharist* (Seabury, 1972), Dr. Massey Shepherd has implied that I did only half a job in explaining why the early admission of children to Communion is a positive step in the appropriate revision of the pattern of Christian nurture. There is, Dr. Shepherd said, the need to examine the question of Confirmation. My thoughts upon reading this review were, in the main, that it was a troublesome task that I did not wish to assume. About the same time, however, I was appointed to the drafting committee on Christian Initiation of the Standing Liturgical Commission of the Episcopal Church, and I found myself involved in the vexed issue of Confirmation whether I desired to be or not.

This book, then, is the result both of a belief that Confirmation is an important issue to the Church and of my experience over the last couple of years attempting to assist the Episcopal Church in preparing liturgical texts in this area appropriate to its needs. It is also an expression of a wider-reaching conviction that ritual is the heart of the community of faith and plays a central role in the way a person lives out his life. Our action is an expression of our perception of the world and that perception, in the final analysis, is always religious. It was Joseph Campbell, the renowned student of mythology, who wrote: "It is the rite, the ritual and its imagery, that counts in religion. . . . A ritual is an organization of mythological symbols; and by participating in the drama of the rite one is brought directly in touch with these."

Therefore, I think the question of how one ritualizes the maturing process, which is the subject of this study, is not a peripheral or esoteric matter. It lies at the heart of growing into complete manhood or womanhood. If it is true, as I believe it is, that the emptiness of life today is partially a result of the lack of symbols operant in our interaction with the world, a ritual such as this book intends by a maturity rite is an important part of helping us grow into a new awareness of our Christian story, in order that we might make it ours.

In previous studies, in which I have sought to examine current religious practice in theological terms, as well as from the data of the human sciences, I have been criticized for being preoccupied with history and abstract analysis. I rather imagine that this book may fall under a similar criticism. This continues to be my approach, however, as a matter of deep-seated conviction. The challenge is before the reader to look at history and to think with me. If he or she disagrees, certainly it needs to be on the same grounds of which the argument is presented.

We live in an ahistorical time. Yet the person who does not know his past does not know who he is. The only way we can live with hope into the future is to know who we are and, from that knowledge, to project our ambitions for ourselves. Otherwise, we are lost in confusion or fantasy or both. The Judaeo-Christian tradition "invented" history, because it was in the light of God's promises in history that we would look with faith to the future. To deny history is to deny our Christian faith.

The person who does not think is destined, as well, to be victimized by the past in the form of undifferentiated feeling, just as the severely neurotic person is captured in the conflicts of his early years that lie buried in his unconscious. Anti-intellectualism has a long and revered American tradition, and has managed to get the Church, as well as the rest of the country, into many a fix. I am confident that no one is converted to the Christian faith on the basis of his powerful thinking; but not a few persons who have thought before they acted have avoided confusing their endocrine glands or their unresolved feelings about their parents with the voice of God.

In this study I have attempted to look at what we are and might possibly be doing in regard to ritualization of the maturing Christian in the light of a reasoned examination of both the history of the Church's practice and the data of anthropology and psychology. Certainly no claims are made to have all the answers or even one or two. My argument is that we need to do everything we can in assisting the maturing process, without limiting ourselves or reducing the mystery of sanctification to a univocal formula. I will be deeply grateful if the book succeeds in only getting the conversation started at a level which does not require doing what we have always been doing because there is nothing better to do, or doing nothing because it is not considered important in our troubled world.

It is impossible to write a study like this without seeming, occasionally if not habitually, polemical. I consider myself fortunate in that I have good friends, for whom I have the greatest admiration, who have taken positions on this matter of Confirmation quite opposed to one another, as well as to me. Among these are not a few bishops, some of whom I think have sometimes let their personal feelings about their role get in the way of the data. However, if I appear polemical, I hope what I say will never be taken personally. The value of a reasoned approach is its ability to search for the truth without offense, because it acknowledges from the beginning that we all have investments as well as fallible minds.

I am particularly indebted in the preparation of this book to a distinguished group of liturgists that I have known over the years: Massey Shepherd, Bonnell Spencer, O.H.C., Thomas Talley, Louis Weil, Daniel Stevick, Leonel Mitchell, Aiden Kavanaugh, O.S.B., and especially Marion Hatchett. The Church in the future will stand very much in the debt of those devoted churchmen and scholars. Dr. Hatchett was kind enough to read the manuscript and save me from some horrendous gaffs, only identifiable to a skilled liturgist like himself. It goes without saying, however, that the opinions in this study are mine and no one else is to be held responsible.

As before, I am grateful to my secretary, Earnest Louise Lumpkins, for typing the manuscript. I wrote this book largely over the Thanksgiving and Christmas holidays, and my family, as always, understood.

Urban T. Holmes
Feast of the Epiphany, 1975

CONFIRMATION

The celebration of maturity in Christ

1

Owning your faith

When I was in seminary one of the issues we discussed at length in pastoral theology was the opinion of those parents who wished to postpone the Baptism of their children "until they made up their own minds." Somehow the integrity of infant Baptism and the Episcopal Church was at stake. We pondered long and hard the appropriate response to this position, and I have from time to time had occasion since to employ the apologetic for infant Baptism which we were then taught. It assumed that one is nurtured in Christ.*

Of course it is true that by the very nature of our humanity no one makes the kind of free decision that those envision who would wait until a person is able to make up his own mind to suggest Baptism. We are our community, particularly when we think of that community as our family; and its commitments and outlook are ours from birth by the very fact of our intimate relationship to it. "To be" is to be in relation. There is no such thing as a human being unattached to that society into which he is born, shaped by its unique perception of the world.

---

* By "nurturing" I do not mean liberating what is already within a person. My understanding of nurture draws from developmental psychology and the theory that a community supports an individual in moving through certain necessary stages in his or her development which must be resolved in relationships.

Erik Erikson, the noted psychoanalyst, has suggested that the critical task of a child's first year of life is his possible orientation to trust or distrust the world, based on his dialogue with that world, beginning with his mother. If this dialogue is resolved in favor of trust he acquires the virtue or strength of hope. "Hope is the enduring belief in the attainability of fervent wishes, . . . the ontogenetic [i.e., having its origin in our being] basis of faith," says Erikson.

Hope is the first and most basic virtue animating man, and is essential for faith in God. The Sacrament of Baptism effects, celebrates, and empowers the child's birth into a community of trust and makes possible his hope in Christ, *once that community into which he is born can rightly be described as "Christian."* * It is altogether appropriate, then, in accordance with what Erikson says about the development of the person, that we should ritually signify this power of hope for the child and his parents.

Baptism is then the experience of birth into the redeeming or hope-giving community of the Church, which parallels the physical birth of the infant into the human family. It gives symbolic expression to what a person is by God's intention, "Christ's own forever," by the very fact of his physical birth. Therefore, it marks the potentiality of every human born into a Christian community.

In face of this truth, however, there is also the conviction that I share with many that each of us has to accept responsibility for what our community has indeed made us; or we have to reject it responsibly for a clear alternative. This is necessary for maturity. If we fail to do

---

* My use of the word "celebrate" in this book is somewhat different than in the now tired aphorism: "celebrate life." I use it more or less as a synonym of "solemnize," as "to solemnize a marriage," meaning to validate or render that which we celebrate.

this we live in a perpetual adolescence. Erikson has said that the last virtue of man—the result of resolving the eighth "crisis" of human development—is wisdom, which involves owning our tradition, which made us what we are. This includes our religion: its heritage and values embodied in its corporate perception of the meaning of our world.

Baptism then signifies our *birth* into the community of Christ, effected by his death and resurrection, but we need to take responsibility—or so it would seem—for what our membership acquired by Baptism means for who we are. It is something like citizenship in a country. I was born an American, but there are times when I must *own* that for myself in concrete acts: getting a social security number, filing a 1040 form with the IRS, registering with the draft board, voting, etc.

This book is concerned with what it means to own that faith into which we were baptized. Baptism itself is a complete act of initiation into the Christian community. This has been expressly stated by the bishops of the Episcopal Church. It needs *nothing* to complete or perfect it as an act of passage into the Church, in spite of some rhetoric or even of teaching to the contrary. Yet maturity in Christ requires an acceptance of responsibility for our socialization from birth within the community of the Church, and that this normally should be ritualized. The question that faces Christians today is how this might best be done: the liturgical expression of our age in the Church.

CONVERSION VERSUS NURTURE

At the beginning of this chapter I said that the assumption is that we are nurtured in Christ. It is the nurturing issue that provokes the question of owning our faith—the faith into which we were baptized. It has to be clear from the start, however, that this makes certain theological claims which are not necessarily explicit in the New Testament. The coming of Christ can be interpreted, and frequently has been, as a call out of this nurturing world, made up of human culture and society. This "call out" I speak of as "conversion." An absolute view, which sees Christian discipleship as this and this alone, is not where I stand, but it is a possible position. This study assumes, to the contrary, that there is a process by which the Christian comes to maturity *within* this world, in which human culture and society are fulfilled by God's grace. This process is one of "nurturing."

In the apostolic Church we do not find Christian families into which children are born and nurtured in Christ.* The committed follower of Jesus in the New Testament is one who has turned from the prevailing paganism or the Jewish establishment as an adult and in his Baptism has sacramentally died to his previous life in this world that he might share in Christ's resurrection into the new world. He is converted. The Cross of Jesus has become the pivotal reality to his new consciousness, and he expects the imminent arrival of the new age.

Writing in the middle of the second century, Justin Martyr describes the meaning and occasion of Baptism. His language is interesting in that it speaks to the intellectual as well as, presumably, the emotional conviction of the convert. It is particularly significant for our thinking in that Baptism is the act of the adult.

I shall now lay before you the manner in which . . . we were made new in Christ. . . . As many as are persuaded and believe

* The position to the contrary of the Swedish scholar, Joachim Jeremias, does not appear to me to be significant or, for my purposes, convincing. He argues largely from texts such as I Cor. 1:16 and Acts 16:15, 33ff.

[6]

that these things which we teach and describe as true, and undertake to live accordingly, are taught to pray and ask God, while fasting, for the forgiveness of sins. . . . They are led by us to a place where there is water, and they are reborn. . . . This washing is called enlightenment, because those experiencing these things have their minds enlightened.

In the mind of Justin, the repentance and rebirth of the sinner into membership in Christ's Body, the Church, is clearly nothing other than the reorientation of the adult consciousness, previously conditioned by a pagan culture, to a life lived in discipleship to Christ. Since for him the mind is identified with the soul, which is the essence of a person, the enlightenment of the mind is a vivid image of God's gift of his new presence in the initiate's life by virtue of his conversion, made effective in his Baptism. It is a movement out of abject darkness into the clear light of day (cf. Jn. 1:3–9).

Another significant point, which Justin illustrates, is the fact that the experience of conversion is seen by the society in which the person lived as culture-denying. Despite his efforts to explain Christianity so that it would be understandable and acceptable to the philosophers of his day, Justin himself was martyred for his faith. Christian Baptism was not an act which celebrated and made effective the socialization process of the individual within the culture of the Roman Empire. It was, on the contrary, a clear threat to that socialization process from the point of view of the society itself. Perhaps the Christians did not always see this as the case, but the Roman authorities did.

This emphasizes what was said at the beginning of the section. In the early Church, Christian initiation was the efficacious celebration of an adult conversion, in which the initiate is seen as called out from the society as a whole. In becoming a member of the Church one made a freely chosen, adult act, which had the effect of excluding oneself from the culture. It was a decisive separation, *by intention*, of the person from the natural processes of acculturation. If it actually did this, I would question how "responsible" that decision might be; but in truth, it is in the final analysis impossible to achieve a complete separation from our socialization within the larger community, and the converted Christian has an appropriate profound influence upon the society as a whole.

Certainly, however, this understanding of initiation has always been an ideal in continuing portions of Christianity, particularly where the experience of conversion and resultant exclusivism have been stressed. There are the examples of the various Anabaptist groups during the Reformation, the pietist communities in the eighteenth century, and the pentecostal movement in this present century. In all such bodies the normative society has been repudiated.*

The Church does not want to get away completely from the norm of adult conversion and Baptism and what this implies for renunciation of the old world. In the current Anglican revisions of the baptismal liturgy, as well as in the Roman Catholic and Lutheran, adult Baptism is seen as normative. Whereas the majority of candidates for Baptism in the Episcopal Church—my own allegiance— are infants, we understand this as a "permissible departure" from the standard, which is the "enlightenment," to

---

* Ernst Troeltsch (1865–1923), a German theologian, coined the terms to distinguish such groups from the more inclusive bodies. The culture-denying groups he called "sects" and those that affirm the culture he called "Churches." In one sense we could say that conversion is expected in the sects and nurture in the Churches.

quote Justin—the current jargon calls it "consciousness raising"—in Baptism of the responsible confessing adult. This is why in the new baptismal liturgy of the Episcopal Church the form for adult Baptism precedes in every case that for infant Baptism. It is also why the renunciations in Baptism have been given a more dramatic emphasis, since there is an implicit assumption that in becoming one with Christ we set ourselves over against something of this world.

Most of us, however, take for granted infant Baptism. Although there is some debate among scholars as to when this practice started in the Church, certainly it had begun to emerge by the late second and into the third centuries. It was not universally accepted until much later. Fourth-century bishops did not baptize their own children, and as late as the eighth century adult Baptism was customary in Spain. Infant Baptism became the norm only in the fifth century. It would seem to me that infant Baptism developed naturally as children were born into Christian families, and was greatly reinforced when the extension of that family, the society itself, was conceived as Christian. The primary symbolism of the Baptism of infants is *in essence* the same as in the Baptism of adults: the initiation into complete membership in Christ's Church. We must acknowledge, however, that the secondary symbolism is very different.

What supported this change was the growing sense of children being *nurtured* in the Christian faith, as I suggested in the beginning of this chapter. Of course, this means the Christian witness lies in a much closer relationship to the prevailing culture than it does in the mind of those who think in terms of conversion from a society of sin and godlessness. There is more of an acceptance of the patterns of this world as those of God.

[9]

What seems then to follow from what we discussed briefly in this section is that there is a problem with the notion of "owning one's faith." I am not backing off from the conviction that in the normal course of Christian nurture we have to take responsibility for our Baptism. What does seem true is that this "normal course of events" implies a process in which as Christians we grow into a kind of maturity in which we are inner-directed or self-authenticating—all "good things" in contemporary humanistic psychology. The problem is that the New Testament notion of conversion implies more a *surrender* or *dying* to self (Mt. 16:24), rather than a process of inner-directed growth. In such death to self one does not "own" anything but, as a child, trusts all to God. I think that any theology of the ritualization of maturity is going to have to keep this contrary perspective in view.

I am suggesting, however, that we not choose sides between the value of *conversion* or *nurture*, as I have outlined them. But it is important that we understand that they are notions indicative of two rather different perceptions of Christian initiation and the relationship of membership in the Church to our presence in a social system beyond the Church, motions which have run parallel to one another in theological thought for over 1700 years. This ambivalence becomes particularly significant when we think of rites of passage and their relationship to owning our faith, which is the subject of the next section. To this point, however, I have sought to provide a basis for understanding something of the incongruent perceptions from which it is necessary to build any concept of the ritualization of the "owning" of one's faith.

In its meeting at Pocono, Pennsylvania, in 1971, the House of Bishops of the Episcopal Church took a look at what they understood to be the nature and purpose of Confirmation. It is my understanding—the official review says nothing—that the report of the Committee on Theology of the House spoke of the need in the course of personal development for a *rite of passage* from childhood or adolescent faith to adult commitment, which the Church ought to provide. This was and is one way of speaking of the ritualization or celebration of the owning of our faith. It is not an idea that originates with the bishops, and it is seen now by many as the best apologetic for the function of Confirmation.

At this point, without looking at the nature of what we call in the Book of Common Prayer "Confirmation" and its relation to the history of sacramental theology, which shall be our task in the second chapter, it is important to look at the meaning of a rite of passage. The term was first given prominence in the work of the French anthropologist, Arnold van Gennep (1873–1957), and he is still considered the principal authority on this subject, even though others have written since on the subject without essentially changing his interpretation.

Van Gennep's discussion of rites of passage is based upon the assumption that ritual serves to maintain the relationships between individuals and groups *within a social system.* In other words, such ritual exists to achieve or prevent transformations of state within the society and its environment in order to make for the best possible social interaction. This is essentially a closed or secular theory of ritual, called structural-functionalism. The function of ritual, this term indicates, is to serve the structures of the society. So when van Gennep speaks of rites of passage he is referring to rituals that have a certain function in effecting transformations of state or status for individuals within a social system. He is saying nothing necessarily about the presence in the ritual of a transcendent being, much less about a God who judges the society and with whom the participant is united by virtue of the ritual or liturgy.

Structural-functionalists are not explicitly denying the existence of God. They are professionally agnostic. There are anthropological theories of ritual which are more congenial to the notion that rites consist of symbols, which do represent and participate in a transcendent reality. These theories provide a clearer conceptual basis for the judgment that ritual does effect a change by God in the lives of its participants; but both they and the structural-functionalists say that rites, whether or not they refer to anyone or anything beyond society, do change people. They nurture members of the culture. They would say that rites of passage, for example, do make possible the passage.* This is a very important point for church people to keep in mind, since I sense a low expectancy of liturgy among many persons very active in their church. Perhaps this is an American prejudice. All the evidence would indicate, however, that where ritual fails, it is not a problem with liturgy as rite *per se*, but with this particular expression of ritual.

* Clifford Geertz, an anthropologist at Princeton University, has claimed in his studies of Javanese society that the cultural structure, of which ritual is a part, exists independently of the social structure, and can be a shaping force in people's lives. This thesis has been supported by the research of Robert Rappaport among New Guinea tribesmen, and in the work of F. E. Errington in the Duke of York Islands. The great bulk of Victor W. Turner's study has shown how ritual orders and motivates the lives of the Ndembu, a people in Tanzania.

There is, of course, a certain tension between the theory that ritual helps maintain the equilibrium of the society, as found in the work of the structural-functionalists, and that it is a source of transsocietal change. At the same time, however, these theories are not mutually exclusive. As I have already suggested in the previous section, religion as conversion stands somewhat opposed to religion as nurture. The former emphasizes our being called out of the world of culture and society, while the latter is comfortably clarified in the theories of the structural-functionalists like van Gennep. I think we have to live with the tension, because both are true: ritual maintains the social system and, at the same time, it calls it into question. A given society's good is not identical with the will of God, but they are not irrevocably opposed either.*

The point has been made that van Gennep says that rites of passage effect a transformation in status for individuals. These rites are observed in various societies at the critical turning points marked by birth, entrance into childhood, social puberty, betrothal, marriage, pregnancy, fatherhood, initiation into religious societies, and death. A status refers, of course, to a person's relationship to others within an institution. It carries with it a set of roles, from which follow society's expectations for observable behavior within that role-set. Therefore, a person participates in a rite of passage at a time when in the course of his development the society imposes a new status and expects different role behavior and responsibility. The ritual effects and celebrates that change. Once the status is conferred *that particular rite of passage is nonrepeatable.* This is important to remember.

* Perhaps the most brilliant analysis of this issue is found in H. Richard Niebuhr's *Christ and Culture* (Harper, 1951). I would recommend this to anyone interested in further investigation.

An illustration of status change is the passage from the status of a minor in the society to that of an adult. In most states a minor is legally not completely responsible for any deviant behavior. If a seventeen-year-old commits a felony, for example, his name does not appear in the paper, he is often tried before a special court, and his sentence is more directed toward reeducation than punishment. It is different if he is eighteen years old. At eighteen his status and therefore the expectations of behavior and responsibility for it changes. This fact might be clearer if we had some ritual more significant than registering for the draft, which applies only to males, to mark the passage.

While there are many rites of passage, according to van Gennep, the one that may apply particularly to owning our faith is that of passage into adulthood. Such rites of passage are *not*, it must carefully be noted, physical puberty rites. Societies that practice rites of passage at this stage rarely if ever identify them with coming to sexual maturity in a physiological sense. They are more appropriately considered under the class of initiation rites into an age group or religious society, which confers a certain status within the social system or religious community. Therefore, it is incorrect to speak of a rite of passage as a puberty rite. Initiation rites, which I have defined here as rites of passage, are particularly significant in societies where the religious community is coterminous with the civil reality.*

A rite of passage, since it involves by definition a change of status and, necessarily, of role—meaning a change in

---

* This is true of what Robert Bellah, an American sociologist, in an essay, "Religious Evolution," calls primitive and archaic religion. It is not so true of historic religion (pre-Reformation Christianity) and certainly not of early modern and modern religion.

our relationships within the institutions (family, government, educational system, Church, etc.) and the expected behavior—effects a change in observable behavior. Van Gennep describes Baptism, particularly as found in the ancient Roman liturgy of the eighth century, as a rite of passage. He can say this because, first of all, it involves the three structural elements of all such rites: separation from the society, a period of transition, and incorporation back into one's new status. It is also true, because Baptism effects an observable change in behavior. One who is baptized stays at the Eucharist, for example, after the dismissal of the catechumens, which was a part of the ancient liturgy. Participation in all the other sacraments is now open to the new member, and he or she is treated as one of the family in a different way than before. If one were not baptized in the eighth century, he or she would also be socially and politically ostracized. Baptism is rightly described there as a rite of passage, particularly when it is part of an ongoing social process.

This leads to another interesting point made by van Gennep. As he says, all rites of passage have a territorial dimension. In these rites, as we cross social thresholds, which are a part of every human community, the passage is expressed in a movement from one place to another. In the ancient Church the pagans were excluded from the church building. Baptism required a movement from one side of the baptistry to the other. We are all generally familiar with the tendency today to put the baptismal font at the door of the church and to see Baptism as the "entrance rite" from which we move to the altar. The revised baptismal liturgy of the Episcopal Church hints at a kind of territorial movement. Space and our location within it has great symbolic power which is integral to a rite of passage.

Van Gennep undoubtedly saw all ritual, however, as too exclusively expressing passage. His book came out in 1908, and in 1942 a helpful further development of ritual classification was offered by two American anthropologists, Eliot Chapple and Carleton Coon. They agreed that there were the rites of passage that van Gennep had identified and that were nonrepeatable celebrations of the passage of the individual through the crises of the developmental cycle, effecting that person's new status in the society. There are also, they said, rites of intensification, which were repeatable celebrations of the group, related to the seasonal cycles, that seek to empower our environment and ourselves within it. Rites of fertility and fecundity, pertaining to agriculture and hunting, would fall within this category. I would emphasize that these rites are less related to the social system and much more to the biological process of human existence.*

Contrary to Chapple and Coon, even these two classifications do not adequately encompass all rituals, nor do they express all theories as to the purpose of ritual. Healing rites, as well as what Max Gluckman, an English anthropologist, calls "rites of rebellion," and the many rites that seek to avoid pollution do not fit either category. Chapple and Coon are in the tradition of structural-functionalism, as well, and these classifications of passage and intensification imply ritual control of our environment rather than openness to the new.

The two anthropologists did, however, succeed in identifying a notable difference: the distinction between rites that effect a once-for-all status change within the social system or the religious community and those rites which

* Chapple and Coon argued that rites of passage had to do exclusively with individuals, and rites of intensification with groups. Later anthropologists have demonstrated that this is not always true on either count.

[16]

intensify or strengthen the relationship between the participant and God.

It follows that rites of passage effect a once-for-all change, principally within the social system. They mark a crisis within the nurturing task of the society. It is a little difficult to think of them as acts of conversion in the sense of a dramatic reversal of one's life-style and a repudiation of the system. Furthermore, when there is no observable behavior change, indicating a change in status within the society or religious community, one cannot rightly speak of a ritual as a rite of passage. If we violate this principle in anthropology we render the category meaningless.

We can, therefore, refer to Baptism as a rite of passage in a clear sense: it celebrates a change in status, always in terms of the religious community and sometimes in terms of the sociocultural world as well. It is of value to be cautious, in another sense, and note that we are stretching the descriptive boundaries a bit, particularly when the Church is unrelated or in a tenuous relationship to the prevailing culture. This was certainly true in the New Testament, where it was an act of conversion rather than a rite of passage within a nurturing process. I am more comfortable in thinking of Baptism as a classical rite of passage the less we emphasize the "otherworldly" dimensions of the rite and the more we let it express the affirmation of a given culture.

It follows from this that the term "rite of passage," which has its origins in a structural-functionalist interpretation of ritual, does not fit comfortably in a community that is anticultural, such as the New Testament Church. Not until the anticulture becomes a counterculture, which it inevitably does, does the term "rite of passage" take on a new reality. Rites of intensification, however, do not have the same problem, because they are not bound to the sociocultural system. They are rooted in natural events and assist the participants in looking beyond the social facts of their existence to the ground of man's being in the order of creation. This fact, together with the emphasis in rites of intensification upon the exchange of power, opens some possibility for interpreting rites of growth in Christ as rituals of intensification. This will be discussed at length in the third chapter.

The concern in this section has been with the possibility of thinking of a ritualization of one's owning his faith as a rite of passage. Just as in the previous section, attention was paid to the tension present in looking at coming to faith in the terms "conversion" and "nurture," so here I am suggesting that there is a tension between ritual that affirms the socially prescribed course of maturation and ritual that transcends the sociocultural systems. This is particularly an issue because rites of passage are related to status-change within the socialization process.

This brings us to the question with which this section opened. Can rites of maturity be considered rites of passage? To answer in the affirmative it would be necessary to show that they effect a clearly defined status-change within the prevailing social system or, at least, within the distinctive subsystem of the institutional Church. The answer is "No" for at least two reasons.

First, there are certainly those who would say that the Church's identification of status is a repudiation of our vocation to transform the world, rather than to be conformed to it (Rom. 12:2). Therefore, a sacramental act which is a rite of passage is for them immediately called in question. Even if I did not agree totally with the implications of this position, there is a great deal to be said for the belief that the Christian faith demands an act of surrender to God just as much as an act of assuming responsibility for maturity in the world, and to own one's faith has to take the former as well as the latter into account.

If we do, however, admit that owning one's faith is at least in part an act of assuming responsibility for the relationship of our Baptism to our life in the present society, it is difficult, secondly, to see just what status-change a maturity rite would effect in our doing this. My reasons for saying this, including the conclusion that rites of passage may actually defeat the Christian maturing process in the contemporary social system, are the subject of the next section.

THE CIVIL AND THE INVISIBLE RELIGION

Robert Bellah wrote in an article, "Civil Religion in America," published originally in *Daedalus* in 1966, as follows:

[We have] from the earliest years of the republic a collection of beliefs, symbols, and rituals with respect to sacred things and institutionalized in a collectivity. This religion—there seems no other word for it—while not antithetical to, and indeed sharing much in common with, Christianity, was neither sectarian nor in any specific sense Christian.

Bellah goes on to say that such a civil religion is alive and well in contemporary America. Furthermore, there are strengths to the civil religion and we should not be altogether despondent over its existence. There have been those who have debated Bellah's thesis in various ways, but generally it seems to have prevailed.

The civil religion is the dominant social system of symbols, if I may define religion in that way, into which we as the citizens of this country are socialized.* Writing about the same time as Bellah, another sociologist, Edgar Friedenberg, made the point that the principal instrument for shaping the citizen of this country into the proper American and, by implication, initiating him into the civil religion, is the public-school system. This is the institution that forms us and educates us into what are the role expectations of the status to which we might be summoned in the society. As we know, that system is something that exists by explicit intention apart from the Church.

Certainly there are various rites of passage within the civil religion—getting a driver's license, making the team or winning some beauty contest, registering for the draft, taking the SAT or ACT and being admitted to a college— but none of them marks in a dramatic, once-for-all manner the movement within such a symbol system from childhood and adolescence into adult status and role expectation. Rather they tend to generate, despite the social activism of the 1960s, a vague feeling that one does not "rock the boat," and to legitimate the inane-to-demonic values given substance in American television. They are "mini-rites of passage" along a process, lasting in various situations from six to twelve years, from age twelve to eighteen or even twenty-five, through which a person

* This is the first part of a definition of religion by Clifford Geertz. The whole definition states that "religion is: (1) a system of symbols which acts to (2) establish powerful, pervasive and long-lasting moods and motivations in men by (3) formulating conceptions of a general order of existence and (4) clothing these conceptions with such an aura of factuality that (5) the moods and motivations seem uniquely realistic." While Geertz is not affirming here the existence of God, but rather describing what he sees in human behavior, this definition is open to the possibility that such a "system of symbols" does indeed enable us to participate in God.

develops his understanding of being an adult in American society. These significant events along the process do communicate some sense of entering a new status, but they also participate in that diffusion which characterizes the American civil religion. What Bellah describes is generally a very weak system of symbols in which there is no significant civil rite of passage.

Our hope would be that the Church would then claim its rightful place and provide a strong system of symbols with its rite of passage, which would motivate us to live as God would have us to do. This would certainly be true if the Church saw herself as opposed to the civil religion. It still holds true when the Church considers herself, as I think she generally does, as in some way partners with the cultural system in this country, and not as converting persons into a counterculture revolutionary group or transculture asceticism. It is noteworthy, for example, that the Southern Baptists, who certainly have a "conversion" theology of initiation, nonetheless are very much in the mainstream of American culture as symbolized in the civil religion. Conversion among the Southern Baptists and many like them is more an expectation within a nurturing process, like that of the more sacramental churches, that removes the once-for-all-ness of conversion. Yet be we Baptist, Episcopal, Roman Catholic, or what have you, we might hope that there could be a way to own one's faith so that he could live in the American system with a greater sense of identity and of doing God's will than is provided in the civil religion.

The fact is that as a general rule the Church does not provide a clear-cut means to own one's faith in such a way that the Christian symbols appear "uniquely realistic" and become a motivating force for a distinctive Christian style of life within the American society. There are undoubtedly a number of reasons for this, but one that seems particularly persuasive is found in the argument of Thomas Luckmann, a German sociologist. To reduce a complicated thesis to a single proposition, he says that there is no single, powerful symbol system—much less Christian—in America that extends much beyond familial communities. In other words, our culture is so fragmented, heterogeneous, and pluralistic that the content of the faith we own is not shared much beyond a group of intimates in any way more than by affirming a belief in the "fatherhood of God and the brotherhood of man." Those by themselves are not very powerful symbols. This situation Luckmann calls the "invisible religion" of Western civilization. There is then no basis for a religiocultural rite of passage.

Initiation into anything more than the civil religion requires a discernible cultural community, which reinforces the values embodied in powerful symbols overtly proclaimed and lived in that community. It demands that we live principally in terms of that system. This is to say that the Amish, for example, are right, as are the Mormons. If a group has any distinctive values it wishes to preserve and by which it is convinced every member must live, then it has to exist to itself as a community. It must protect its members from the more diffuse, larger society, otherwise it too becomes "invisible." Otherwise, a powerful motivating system of symbols can exist in our culture only in natural groups, such as the family. We are too diverse, too fragmented, too heterogeneous for anything else. This diffusion could be considered a virtue, as some consider it.

Erik Erikson, for example, has argued that in our complex society, with the many and varied role-expectations facing us all, symptomatic of a spectrum of often conflicted statuses, adolescence requires a certain moratorium. This is a time for integrating the elements of their identity gained in the past and for testing perceived values and possible patterns of action within the society as a whole and the cultural community of which they would be a part. Anyone who has had adolescent children, as I have, knows both the inevitability of this kind of behavior in our society and its frightening dimensions. We can never be certain in which cultural context their search will be resolved, or if it will find resolution at all. Erikson's point is that the process must go on if an adolescent is to be a creative adult. My point would be that such a moratorium is the exact opposite of owning of one's faith in a once-for-all rite of passage, which would defeat what Erikson describes as a desirable experimental relationship to status and role in our society.

Erikson is describing a process that begins with an internal turmoil and journey and moves on, never ending in the final sense in which the individual commits himself to a community of faith and value. Even this commitment is subject to constant renegotiation because both the social and cultural systems into which we are inevitably thrust change in all but the most primary ways. Therefore, owning one's own faith has to be done again and again, for it is not simply reinforced, but it is continually challenged.* The challenge makes for a world where greater freedom and creativity are possible than in a more homogeneous society, but also makes for a greater risk.

Every time someone moves in America his faith is

* What I have in mind here finds a close parallel in John Snow's book, *On Pilgrimage: Marriage in the 70s* (Seabury, 1971), p. 143. "The pilgrim marriage is episodic. It does not strain to remain the same but is open and responsive to new people and events which must be met as the couple moves not so much through time as with it."

challenged. We have to reestablish our community of faith, for no two congregations in the most monolithic denomination are perceived as the same. Each new job questions our identity and therefore our values. We have to find our power anew. Time itself brings change, in which, if we are not constantly discerning once more the symbols of God's presence in our life, we are liable to find ourselves bereft of any living content to our life. Our personal relations come and go, perhaps even to the depth of our marriage, and consequently the self we once knew in the reflection of others is challenged by what we see in new relationships. Faith does not exist in a vacuum. It is in some sense a function of our social selves, as I hope this chapter has made self-evident. If we are to own the faith into which we were born at our Baptism, we have to do so again and again, in small and large ways, but all qualitatively the same. Paradoxically, it always involves an element of surrender: giving over the ownership to God. For the Christian it is an assertion that he owns a dual citizenship consistent with the Incarnation: a citizenship both in heaven and on earth.

SUMMARY

What I have sought to do in this chapter is to explore under the notion of "owning your faith" some anthropological and sociological considerations in how a mature Christian may go about taking responsibility for his Baptism. I am concerned for the best way to celebrate this "owning" liturgically or sacramentally. What may be a basic source of confusion for the reader, but a necessary consideration, is a prevailing countertheme throughout the chapter, in which I question the *all-encompassing* value of the image of owning your faith. This phrase assumes an element of control in our Christian witness, an authentication of self within the Christian community, that must be held in tension with the fact that fulfillment in Christ is symbolized by the Cross, life found in human impotence. Faith is an act of surrender, a death to self, and to be a baptized person is to give ourselves over to an experience in which we remain childlike.

Having introduced this opposing theme, I have sought to explore the initial proposition, the need to take responsibility for our Baptism, and have developed the following points which are important for the rest of this study.

First, granting that Baptism is a sacramental action within a nurturing Christian community—an assumption open to question—it is a rite of passage in van Gennep's sense. It effects through separation, transition, and incorporation a change in status for the initiate, as defined by the religious community and in terms of the socialized developmental cycle of the individual. This is in spite of and not because of the effete way we celebrate the baptismal rite in the Church today. That status is full membership in the Church of Christ.

Second, rites of passage are nonrepeatable and are tied to the social system. The status conferred is defined by the cultural and/or social system, including the religious community; and once given, it is the possession of the individual. Hence Baptism is nonrepeatable. There are other rituals, called rites of intensification, which do not confer status but are a source of power. These are not tied to social definitions of status and can be repeated.

Third, in our American social system there is no one moment in which an adolescent enters a clearly defined adult status by any cultural or social system. Within the many cultural options and without a clear social support, there is no symbol system of any clarity and compulsion beyond our familial communities. Adolescence is therefore a long *process* of testing our identity, even as Christians within various cultural options, in which maturity is achieved within a continuum.

Fourth, if the Church is to relate its sacramental life to the developmental cycle of the individual within his community—which is not an unquestionable approach—there is no basis for *one nonrepeatable rite of passage* into the adult age group within our cultural and social system. The process of maturation is too episodic in America. The process of coming of age in America suggests a ritualization more akin to rituals of intensification, empowering the churchman to pursue his quest for his identify as a maturing person in Christ.

This fourth point requires that we relate the cultural and social definition of adulthood to the Church's understanding of a responsible member of the Body of Christ. This is a subject for the rest of this book. What I hope to have accomplished at this point is to have moved our thinking from too easy an equation between what Christians do in late-twentieth-century America to own their faith and what Australian aborigines did to make boys into men since the dawn of history. I have heard some argue that their part of this country is culturally closer to prehistoric Australia than suburban Los Angeles, but certainly we cannot reflect on liturgy in terms of anything but the prevailing climate of America.

Perhaps it is now obvious that owning your faith today is a very complex and tenuous process, somewhat questionable in its biblical roots when considered alone, and certainly not reducible to unexamined application of traditional procedures. Let us now examine, however, that practice of the Christian past.

2

A rite in search of a reason

The issue is Confirmation. I have purposely avoided, where possible, pointing to the place of the traditional Confirmation rite in the first chapter, because I wished to begin to build some basis for owning our faith in the anthropological understanding of man's religious life before calling up the feelings that many have identified with Confirmation. Certainly to many churchmen, however, the Confirmation rite as we know it in the Book of Common Prayer has always existed as the means for a person to ritualize his coming of age in the Church. Its title indicates something of this purpose: "The Order of Confirmation or the Laying on of Hands upon those that are Baptized, and come to Years of Discretion." "Years of Discretion" imply a moment within the nurturing process when a person can take an adult responsibility for his baptismal vows.

Liturgical revision in the Anglican Communion and beyond has given expression, however, to a questioning concerning Confirmation that has gone on for at least a generation among theologians. The immediate and straightforward assumption that Confirmation is and always has been the Church's maturity rite has been challenged, largely as its relation to Baptism has been brought into question. Perhaps the average churchman, clerical or lay, is not aware of the heated debates that have raged over the gift of the Holy Spirit in Baptism as compared to Confirmation: a debate which some would probably dismiss as "nit-picking." This argument does have direct implications, however, for our understanding of Christian initiation, which is a much larger and more important issue. It also brings into question some of the traditional assumptions in regard to Confirmation as a rite celebrating Christian maturity.

Anglican theologians have in the past stated, without any support other than nine hundred years of English tradition, that one has to be confirmed to be admitted to Communion. This is an issue of Christian initiation; and as most of us know it is an unique claim of Anglicanism that we are now rapidly and happily surrendering with the admission of young, unconfirmed children to Communion. Anglicanism has always stood with the 1500-year tradition of the universal Church that one does not have to be confirmed "to be saved," but until now has certainly implied the opposite by requiring it for admission to Communion. In reversing our stand we have acknowledged something of what we no longer believe Confirmation to be in the course of becoming a member of the Church. What that "something" was remains a bit of a mystery, since in requiring Confirmation as the prerequisite for Communion no one had ever quite stated what made the laying on of hands by a bishop necessary.* The

* C. B. Moss in *The Christian Faith: An Introduction to Dogmatic Theology* (SPCK, 1943), p. 349, makes the incredible statement, which is logically absurd: "It is of the utmost importance that this rule [that only the confirmed be admitted to Communion] be rigidly observed, because the baptism of infants is

argument tended more to focus on pre-Confirmation instruction and the need "to understand what we are doing." No one to my knowledge ever claimed that Confirmation itself imparted this enlightenment, that is, as doctrinal content or meaning, which is not what Justin Martyr meant in using the terms of Baptism.

Of course, there are undoubtedly some who feel Confirmation is *not* an issue because it is a dominical given. It is, they would say, one of the seven sacraments, ordained in some sense by Christ. Acts 8:14–17 is used to prove its scriptural base. Certainly those who argue this way are aware that the seven sacraments were defined as such by the Western Church in 1215 at the Fourth Lateran Council, after almost twelve hundred years of existence. They would insist probably that what was always implicit at that time became finally explicit in 1215, with a good number of centuries of practical experience of the Sacrament of Confirmation having gone on before.

I do not wish to attack the sacramental character of what we have known in the Church as Confirmation, leaving aside for the moment the question as to whether what we call Confirmation has always been the same thing. My point here is that, if we can do no more than cite the historic sacramental rite of Confirmation, our answer to the question of how the adult liturgically accepts responsibility for his faith fails. The rite is indeed historic, but it carries a great deal of traditional "baggage," some of which raises serious problems for any purpose relating to maturity rites. It is important, therefore, that we examine the data concerning Confirmation in this chapter and discover for ourselves whether it is the answer to the contemporary need to ritualize the owning of our faith.

---

often so indiscriminately administered that we cannot treat it as always conferring real membership."

In Acts we are told that the apostles heard that Samaria had accepted the word of God, and that they sent two of their number, Peter and John, to visit them. Their two representatives learned that the Samaritans had only been baptized "into the name of the Lord Jesus, that and nothing more. So Peter and John laid their hands on them and they received the Holy Spirit" (8:16–17). During all of our lifetime we have read this passage in the Book of Common Prayer—even though it was first introduced as an option no earlier than 1892—and everyone has assumed that here was the scriptual authority for Confirmation. There are good reasons now for believing that this is not such an authority.

In reading the Scriptures we cannot choose one passage that suits our purpose and read into it a contemporary meaning. We have to compare what goes on before and after that passage, as well as the whole of the book, in order to understand as best we can what the author is saying to the reading public he envisions. Obviously Luke is not giving liturgical directions here or outlining a sacramental theology, both of which emerged centuries later. As far as he is concerned, the Holy Spirit comes at Baptism (Acts 2:38;19:5–6); or even before Baptism (Acts 10:44–48) as well as after Baptism. His concern in this passage is with who has the power of being an instrument in the gift of the Holy Spirit: intinerant miracle workers, unlicensed healers, self-appointed evangelists—all epitomized in the figure of Simon the Magician. This was a vital issue to a struggling little Church seeking to establish its authority. Luke's answer is that the Church has the power, which he illustrates in this account. Since Luke, and probably he alone of the New Testament authors, conceives of the Twelve as the embodiment of the Church—there is very little mention of the Twelve Apostles *per se* anywhere in the New Testament except in the two books by Luke—it is only natural that he recount how two of the Twelve who are the symbol of the new Israel bestow the Holy Spirit upon the Samaritans, who were as yet without the Spirit.

What about the laying on of hands in this passage? Anglicans particularly are prone to jump immediately to the conclusion that here we have the proper matter ("the outward and visible sign") of the Sacrament of Confirmation. Again, this is not tenable. In both the Old and New Testament the laying on of hands was a natural act of blessing, by which act of physical contact the person performing same was acknowledging the other in the presence of God. It expresses or effects a flow of power. In the Old Testament it is used to transfer guilt (Lev. 16:20–22, Susanna 34) or to identify with the sacrificial offerings (Lev. 1:4, 3:2, 4:4; Num. 8:12). In the Acts of the Apostles it is also used, as in the rabbinical practice, as a means to ordain (6:6), to heal (9:12, 17, 28:8), and even to commission people for a journey (13:3). In the early Church it is used for exorcism, for the reception of penitents, and in the Sacrament of Penance. I emphasize this because in the Episcopal House of Bishops there is some opinion that the laying on of hands must be carefully prescribed for a few limited sacramental acts.

If we look for the beginning of something the Church had historically called "Confirmation," we have to begin later than the New Testament. A good place to start would be with *The Apostolic Tradition of Hippolytus*, a writing whose original dates from about A.D. 215. Hippolytus was a bishop of Rome. Among other things, his writing describes a Baptism, probably in the tradition of that city.

In this rite the bishop presides. The rite begins with exorcisms by the bishop with the laying on of hands. The candidate strips and then moves to an anointing by a presbyter, assisted by two deacons, with what is called the "oil of exorcism," at the time of the renunciations. This is followed by the naked candidate being led down into the water by a deacon and dipped or immersed, as a presbyter by the side of the water asks him to profess the baptismal creed (which we know as the Apostles' Creed) in a manner found in the revised baptismal liturgy of the Episcopal Church. Once the newly baptized comes up out of the water he is anointed again, presumably by a presbyter, with the "oil of thanksgiving." These two anointings, the oil of exorcism and of thanksgiving, are in fact one and are called the first baptismal anointing. The candidate is then clothed and led to the bishop, who lays his hands upon him and prays for the gift of the Holy Spirit, pours over him consecrated oil or chrism (oil mixed with balsam), and then lays his hands upon him again, saying, "I anoint thee with holy oil in God the Father Almighty and Christ Jesus and the Holy Ghost." This is called the second baptismal anointing or the *sphragis* (meaning the anointing *par excellence*).

The whole of this action is Baptism or initiation: stripping, renunciations with anointing, immersion or dipping naked in the water, anointing as one arises from the water, clothing, and being led to the bishop for laying on of hands, chrismation, and prayer. There is no reason to think that Hippolytus made any kind of distinction within this total action as to when the person became renegerate, his sins were removed, he was reborn, and the Holy Spirit came to him. Third-century man did not think that way. It had to be left to thirteenth-century man to analyze and distinguish. Baptism was seen as a single unified action of Christian initiation.

Hippolytus is, of course, a representative of the Western Church. It is interesting that in the Eastern Church there is no evidence of any postbaptismal anointing prior to the last half of the fourth century. The laying on of hands in the East refers to pushing the person down under the water. It is the contact between the West and the East, brought about by the tourist traffic to Jerusalem in the post-Constantinian Empire, that apparently introduced such customs in the Eastern Church.

To my knowledge, the first Eastern sources in which the postbaptismal anointing occur are the writings of St. Cyril of Jerusalem and the *Apostolic Constitutions*, a document probably Syrian in origin. They both date from the late fourth century. In their description of the second baptismal anointing we find a very interesting thing. There is no mention of the bishop *necessarily* presiding. The anointing at the time of the renunciations remains, and the immersion or dipping in the water follows. However, the anointing after the newly baptized comes up out of the water is now the second baptismal anointing, the pouring of the chrism. It can be done by a presbyter. The effect is seen as the same. As a matter of fact, St. Cyril puns on the word "chrism," telling the newly baptized that they are now "Christs." This is true, he says, by the candidates "receiving the emblem of the Holy Ghost." For, as he continues, "the Holy Ghost in substance rested upon him [Christ]," when he came up out of the water of Baptism, and so the candidates are "given the unction, the emblem of that wherewith Christ was anointed; and this is the Holy Ghost."

What happened to the bishops? The answer is that from

the third century on, with the number of baptismal candidates greatly increasing in proportion to the number of bishops, it became increasingly difficult for a bishop to be present at all Baptisms. Baptisms are still reserved for Easter and possibly a few other great feasts, increasing the need for more *places* of Baptism, rather than *occasions*. The problem is further magnified because, as I said in the previous chapter, infant Baptism now becomes a growing practice. So, just as the bishops bestowed the authority to preside at the Eucharist on the presbyters (thereby giving presbyters the title of "priest"), they also bestowed the authority to preside at Baptism. This became consolidated in the fourth century when, with the recognition of the Church by the Roman state, the Baptisms increased even more and bishops became more occupied as part of the civil bureaucracy.

In the East this authority to preside at Baptisms carried the power to confer the second baptismal anointing or the *sphragis*. As we have read, here the candidate is sealed or marked, just as a slave was branded, not only as belonging to Christ, but as *a* "Christ," an "anointed one" himself, a "Christian." The chrism came to be blessed by a bishop, but its use in Baptism was employed by a priest in his absence. It might be helpful to look ahead here and note that this sealing is clearly restored to its original place in the revision of the baptismal liturgy of the Episcopal Church, and may be done by a priest. I shall argue—if this seems so very novel—that the priest in the Anglican Communion has conferred the *blessing* of the second baptismal anointing or *sphragis* at Baptism since 1549.

In the West the greatly increased number of Baptisms in proportion to the bishop's time was handled differently, *and this is the source of the Confirmation issue.* St. Cyprian,

Bishop of Carthage in the mid-third century, wrote a colleague named Jubalianus: "They who are baptized in the Church are brought to the prelates of the Church, and by our prayers and by imposition of the hand obtain the Holy Spirit, and are perfected [*consummantur*] with the Lord's seal." * Cyprian does not mention chrismation here, although he does say in another letter that chrism is necessary that "he may be the anointed of God and have in him the grace of Christ." The technical use of the term "chrism" for the Western rite of sealing by the bishop was not yet clear, and so we do not know if Cyprian was referring to the first or second baptismal anointing. By the time of St. Augustine of Hippo in the early fifth century, it is obvious that chrismation is a separate sacramental act in the life of the Western Church, of which a bishop is the most appropriate minister. The laying on of hands seems to take second place to the distinctive sacramental imagery in this rite of the chrism.

The West, therefore, solved the problem of the shortage of bishops at Baptisms in a different way from the East. They waited until later, when a bishop was available, to bring the baptized to be sealed. In solving the liturgical problem, however, they created a theological problem. For whether the form of the sacramental actions was the laying on of hands, chrismation, or both, they were completing a *rite,* which for historical reasons could not be finished as it had been before in the days of Hippolytus. The Church's memory is short, however, and this fragment of ritual action cried out for an integrity of its own.

* Cornelius, Bishop of Rome and a contemporary of Cyprian, is recorded as having questioned the priesthood of an opponent, Novatian, on the grounds that he was baptized, but never sealed by a bishop. "Sealing" does not necessarily imply chrism at that time.

In search for that integrity it should be very clear that at this point in time—the end of the ancient world and the beginning of the heroic age of the medieval world—we do not have in chrismation some kind of conscious maturity rite. Some people in recent years have seen in Confirmation a parallel with the Jewish rite of *bar mitzvah*, when at the age of thirteen a Jewish boy becomes legally responsible under the covenant. *Bar mitzvah* means "son of the covenant." There is even an occasional person who interprets Jesus' visit to the Temple (Lk. 2:41–52) as his *bar mitzvah*, which suggests that Confirmation finds a scriptural warrant in the boyhood of Jesus, and that Confirmation was done through the centuries with this in mind.

Actually the story of Jesus in the Temple is an adaptation of a common ancient tale, which was told of Moses, Josephus (a Jewish writer of the first century), Cyrus of Persia, Alexander the Great, Apollonius (an ancient philosopher and miracle worker), and Setme Chamois (son of Rameses II of Egypt). It also occurs as a Chinese legend. It appears in Luke apparently as a product of the first-century Hellenistic-Jewish Christian community, and is therefore a gentile story with an Old Testament coloring. It is recounted to assure the readers of the surprising wisdom of Jesus at a young age and to suggest an early prediction of his religious destiny. It has nothing to do with a *bar mitzvah*, much less Confirmation.

The ritual of *bar mitzvah* itself is no older than the fifteenth century. It is true that in the second-century writings of the Jewish rabbis it is said that a boy reaches legal responsibility for at least some things at age thirteen, but there is no ritual of which we know to celebrate this fact. Therefore, it would be an anachronism to draw any parallels between Confirmation, Luke, and the *bar mitzvah.*

In fact, when medieval bishops did chrismate their people, which was observed more in the breach, it could be an action of no greater distinction than the anointing of an infant or child held up to the bishop as he passed through his immense diocese on horseback. Bishops were required to visit each parish in their diocese every three years, but this was for the purpose of preaching and sitting in judgment. It was the teaching and juridical office of the bishop that was emphasized, and not the sacramental.

There is little reference to Confirmation at all in the records. Where it is mentioned, however, it is the chrism which the bishop or his attendants carried with him, that is the matter of the sacramental act. The Latin writings of the fourth through sixth centuries do speak of the "imposition of *a* hand," undoubtedly in conjunction with the act of chrismation. After the sixth century, mention of the laying on of a single hand, much less "hands," does not appear in the documents until the fourteenth century.* The reader needs, therefore, to avoid imposing his image of Confirmation upon the medieval practice as an act where the candidate kneels before the bishop to receive the "laying on of hands," following some kind of preparation.

If we can show that the early medieval Church did not conceive of this rite as a maturity rite, akin to the Jewish *bar mitzvah,* we do have to admit at the same time that some were to explain its purpose in other terms, which

* The 1928 *Book of Common Prayer*, following the ancient custom, mentions only *a* hand, contrary to the usual practice of hand*s*. Some older pictures and statues of Anglican bishops show one hand on the head of the candidate and the other hand uplifted in prayer at the time of the laying on of hands.

eventually did suggest a maturity rite. The detached "second baptismal anointing" was called from the third century the *consummatio* or *perfectio,* meaning "completion." The reference was undoubtedly to the completion of the literary and ceremonial form of the initiation rite, seen in its entirety in the liturgy of Hippolytus. It was very easy for the notion of completion to slip over, however, to the *effects* of the rite, and to speak of chrismation by a bishop as a "completion" of what Baptism began. This is most important to note, because in this lies much of our problem.

Certainly with the strong feeling of the centrality of the bishop in the Christian community common to the late ancient Church, the fact that the bishop was not present at all Baptisms left people with a sense of something lacking. This would reinforce the notion that the ritual was not "complete," which feeling was resolved in the Western Church by having the bishop "perfect" the ritual. The problem was in developing a theological rationale for the completion of a once-for-all passage from outside the Christian community into its membership. How is it possible to say that after Baptism a person is a member of the Body of Christ, but not quite? This sums up the theological issue.

The word "confirmation" is from the Latin *confirmatio,* and was first used in the fifth century by a Gallican preacher, probably Faustus of Riez (c. 408–c. 490). Interestingly enough, Faustus was an opponent of Augustine of Hippo in that he argued that the initial progress toward salvation could be made on the strength of the human will, rather than requiring the power or grace of God from the beginning. (This is called semi-Pelagianism.) The word *confirmatio* or confirmation, as used by Faustus, is roughly a synonym for *consummatio* or *perfectio,* meaning "completion." We must be careful not to see this term at this date in some technical or narrow sense. If chrismation was described as the confirmation or completion of Baptism, in some liturgies as late as the eleventh century the chalice communicated to the newly baptized was also called the *confirmatio* or confirmation. The word generally described the completion of a liturgical action and, by implication, possibly its effects.

Faustus would have been about thirty-three when the Synod of Orange met in southeastern France to decide some issues for the Church in southern France and northern Italy. Among them was a controversy over chrismation. The decisions of the synod included the statement that a priest may, in the absence of a bishop, chrismate the baptized; and, it is added that the bishops need to supply the priests with chrism.* It is also stated in a rather obscure text that chrismation should not be repeated; although this cryptic statement follows: "A repetition of the anointing has indeed nothing against it, but is not necessary."

Pope Gregory II (669–731), in writing Boniface, the evangelist to the Germans, answered several of his questions about appropriate practice in his work. One answer stated that chrismation is done only once. It is interesting that, as apparently was true of the participants at the Synod of Orange, the question was asked, reflecting a desire for the repetition of chrismation on the part of some persons. Pope Gregory II gives no reason for his answer, and we can only assume that he is representing the tradition.

That tradition has frequently been traced to the discus-

* It should be noted, in passing, that this is precisely what is proposed in the *baptismal* liturgy of the Episcopal Church.

sion of Augustine of Hippo concerning chrismation in a letter to Petilian, a Donatist heretic. Augustine described chrismation in the imagery of Moses anointing Aaron priest (Lev. 8:1–13). The anointing perfects, he says, the Christian in his faith; it is the "ointment of unity," which is an altogether fitting image in writing a Donatist. The crucial passage in his statement is that the sacrament of chrism is a kind of visible sign, "like Baptism itself." Since in other writings Augustine has carefully defended the nonrepeatability of Baptism, many scholars would assume that this is what he intends for Petilian to understand for chrismation. If this is so, it is difficult to see what the theological significance supporting this might be, unless we assume with some scholarship of a generation ago that the "perfecting" of chrismation is, in fact, the completion of a kind of halfway initiation achieved in Baptism.

The early Middle Ages are marked by a rather unreflective acceptance of the tradition, with the added confusion caused by the influx of a northern European outlook. It is well known how the Germanic world view redirected the emphasis in the Eucharist from the action of the sacred meal to the objective nature of the sacred species of Bread and Wine. It also caused some new emphases in the relation of Baptism and Confirmation. For example, Rabanus Maurus (776 or 784–856), Archbishop of Mainz, and described as "one of the greatest theologians of his age," considered Confirmation a more significant rite than Baptism, because its minister was more important and it involved a "worthier" part of the body, the forehead. Fortunately, this kind of argument did not prevail, but it reflects the kind of piety upon which the later scholastics had to build.

The average Christian today undoubtedly has little grasp of how much his world view, not only as a churchman but as a member of Western civilization, owes to scholasticism. It was through the development of a rigorous intellectual methodology by the medieval school-men, which reached its height in the twelfth and thirteenth centuries, that a whole analytical approach emerged that gave birth to modern science. For the first few centuries of its existence the energies of scholasticism were directed to an understanding of revealed truths, and therefore we see for the first time an attempt to unfold the reason behind the tradition of such things as chrismation.

Peter Lombard (c.1100–1160) was the author of the standard scholastic theology textbook of the Middle Ages, the *Sentences*. The first serious attempt at a sacramental theology appears in his writings, and therefore it is most important to see what he said about Confirmation, which he describes as the act of signing the baptized "on the forehead with sacred chrism." The proper minister is a bishop, he argues, because the Scriptures say so. The "virtue" of the sacrament is "the gift of the holy spirit for strength, who is given in baptism for remission." This distinction between strengthening and remission becomes most important. Confirmation is not to be repeated, says Peter Lombard, because it would do "injury" to a sacrament if "we were to repeat what must not be repeated"—which is obviously a circular argument.

Peter Lombard was really the first person to crystallize the notion of seven sacraments, including Confirmation. At the Fourth Lateran Council (1215) they were so defined. Shortly after that, Thomas Aquinas (c.1225–1274), the preeminent philosopher and theologian of the Church, wrote about Confirmation. In all his writings he said that this sacrament is one of "spiritual growth," which bestows the "perfection of spiritual strength . . . when a man dares to confess his faith in Christ in the presence of anyone, whosoever it be." "By the sacrament of Confirmation man is given a spiritual power in respect of sacred actions other than those in respect of which he receives power in Baptism." The distinction lies in the difference between being "a soldier of Christ's faith" and engaging in "spiritual combat" on the one hand, and in being forgiven and regenerate on the other hand. This metaphor of chrismation making one a "soldier of Christ" is important for the Anglican understanding of the initiation rites.

While there is in Aquinas the persistent image of perfection, along with strengthening as seen in Peter Lombard, there is also more than a hint of Confirmation as a kind of maturity age. The Christian is strengthened in his faith, Aquinas says, when he comes to a "perfect age," so that he may be a soldier for Christ. "Perfect age" means maturity in the sense of being completely developed in body and mind. He does not say when that is, and since Confirmation was bestowed in some places in the late Middle Ages as early as age seven, we cannot be sure whether Aquinas was taken seriously. It should be noted, in passing, however.

Aquinas also argues in a significant way that, along with Baptism and Ordination, Confirmation imparts "character." The original Greek word *charaktēr,* from which we get the English, means an imprint, like the image on a coin; and the implication of the word is that of an indelible stamp, making the object what it is (like the minter's die, which makes a piece of silver into the coin of the realm). In theology the notion, if not the term, appears in an early, distinct form in the writings of Augustine of Hippo, who speaks of the "consecration" or "dominical sign" imparted by Baptism, making one a member of the Church no matter what the moral substance of its minister. It was the authority of Innocent III (1160–1216), the pope of the Fourth Lateran Council, who more than 750 years later made the specific term of "character" integral to sacramental theology.

It was not until the Council of Trent (1545–1563), a synod of the Roman Catholic Church called in opposition to the Reformation and bearing no authority whatsoever in Anglicanism, that sacramental character was declared a dogma and that Confirmation, along with Baptism and Ordination, imparted character and was therefore unrepeatable. Aquinas has defined character as a "spiritual power ordained to certain sacred actions." Trent did not do as well as this, saying only that character is a "spiritual and indelible sign," imparted in Confirmation by chrism used by a bishop alone. Trent did go on to say that Confirmation was *not* just an occasion for adolescents to own their faith, as some Reformers did. So with Trent we come to a clear juridical definition of chrismation, as the Sacrament of Confirmation, but the theology of the rite still seems vague.

THE ANGLICAN COMPROMISE

The understanding of Confirmation in the English Church has always been a rather singular one. English society, both in its local form and exported form, has seemed rather fond of structure. Confirmation has been a valuable aid for a long time in the structuring of the piety of Anglicans.

It began with John Peckham (c.1225–1292), Archbishop of Canterbury, who was appointed by the pope with orders to enforce the Gregorian reforms in that uncivilized frontier land. This he did, seeking among other things to put the parishes of the nation under the clear control of the bishops, over whom he held sway. To this end, in 1285 he directed that no one could make their Communion until they were confirmed by a bishop: a regulation without precedent and theologically impossible to defend (as one may judge by the contradictions in the arguments of those who do). The second rubric after Confirmation in the Book of Common Prayer (page 299) remains as a monument to Peckham's use of the sacraments for purposes of ecclesiatical discipline.

Peckham's successor by almost three hundred years, Thomas Cranmer (1489–1556), apparently saw no great problems in this legislation, for reasons that I shall suggest in a moment. In preparing the first Book of Common Prayer in 1549 Cranmer did do something quite novel and most remarkable, however, which we Anglicans generally fail to notice. Confirmation, as we have seen, was the name given to the "second baptismal anointing," which began to detach itself from Baptism in the third century. In the thirteenth century Aquinas described the effect of this anointing with chrism as making the mature person a "soldier of Christ." What Cranmer did was *return* the "second baptismal anointing" and its Thomistic interpretation to Baptism.

This is so often unnoticed that I need to emphasize what is being said. The action of chrismation, identified by the Church for twelve hundred years as Confirmation, was collapsed by Cranmer back into Baptism. This chrismation always followed the actual dipping of the candidate in the water, until it was postponed to wait for a bishop. But Cranmer would no longer postpone it. In the 1549 Book of Common Prayer it was required that the candidate be signed on the forehead with chrism immediately after dipping. The 1552 Book of Common Prayer, which was more influenced by the Protestant Reformation, dropped the use of chrism; but it added, most interestingly, a prayer that picks up the theology of Aquinas in regard to Confirmation by chrismation.

We receive this child into the congregation of Christ's flock, and do sign him with the sign of the cross, in token that hereafter he shall not be ashamed to confess the faith of Christ crucified, and manfully *to fight under his banner against sin, the world, and the devil, and to continue Christ's faithful soldier* and servant unto his life's end (emphasis added).

The matter, form, and intent of the ancient sacrament of Confirmation now became an integral part once again of the baptismal liturgy. Only the minister of the sacrament was changed.

Yet we all know there is a rite of Confirmation from the beginning in the Book of Common Prayer. Is this a different rite by the same name? To attempt to understand what may have happened, several things have to be kept in mind. First, there seems to be some reason to believe that in the late medieval Church there was a renewed concern for the laying on of hands or just one hand, particularly in Confirmation. At least, reference to it appears again in the liturgical books used by bishops of the Roman rite, as well as in the practice of some of the reform movements (such as Wyclif and Hus). Secondly, there is a growing obsession in the Western Church, which reaches a climax in the sixteenth century, for the necessity of intellectual understanding for a worthy participation in worship and the Christian life. Catechisms, sermons, education of the clergy, and long exhortations before prayer are characteristic of this deep concern for knowing what one is doing. Third, in England there was a great debate over the sacramental nature of Confirmation. Cranmer was one who did not consider Confirmation a sacrament, but he was enough of a politician to realize the need to maintain a certain ambiguity in the liturgy.

What we find in the Book of Common Prayer is a compromise. The bishop is retained as a minister of a ritual act, which by 1552 consisted solely of the laying on of hands. The original version, 1549, also had a signing *without* chrism, but that was dropped. The very title of the rite in 1549, "Confirmation, wherein is contained a catechism for children . . ." indicates its purpose: the celebration of the owning of one's faith after instruction.* That instruction is fulfilled when a child—and children are seen as the proper recipients—can recite the Lord's Prayer, the Apostles' Creed, and the Ten Commandments. The emphasis is on a kind of reasoned grasp of the faith. In 1662 the title of Confirmation is expanded to read: "Or laying on of Hands upon Those that are Baptized and come to Years of Discretion" emphasizing even more that this service is seen as a maturity rite, which in good sixteenth- and seventeenth-century tradition would be perceived as acquiring a minimal intellectual grasp of the faith.

The prayer that accompanies the laying on of hands is a 1552 composition: "Defend, O Lord, this thy child with thy heavenly grace, . . ." ** There was no prayer for the laying on of hands in the medieval and ancient Church. This prayer and the one for the Holy Spirit, which precedes it, emphasize the notion of the Holy Spirit strengthening and preserving the Christian as he grows in holiness. There is no implication of any status-change:

* In his writings Cranmer speaks of Confirmation as being administered at a "perfect age," which is the same phrase found in Aquinas.

** Bishop John Cosin (1594–1672), who had a great deal to do with the 1662 revision of the *Book of Common Prayer*, described this prayer as ill-befitting the action of a bishop.

even that of becoming a "soldier for Christ." Clearly the order of Confirmation was, in the minds of Cranmer and those who followed, a service that provided a structure for the education of the children in that knowledge which was deemed necessary for the soul's health. This intention was a part of the outlook of modern rationalism.

This is confirmed in what the seventeenth-century Caroline divines say. They were interested in avoiding the superstitions of Rome, but they still wanted to hold to the value of what was called "bishoping." The truth of the matter seems to be that, while it was considered a "good thing," no one was particularly excited about it. Richard Baxter (1615–1691) described in a charming manner how at age fifteen he was "bishoped" with thirty to forty others on the spur of the moment in the churchyard, having had no instruction and not even knowing what the bishop was saying. It is obvious that for almost two centuries (1607–1785) Anglicans in this country, lacking a bishop, were never confirmed unless they journeyed to England. The addition in 1662 to the second Confirmation rubric of the words "or ready and desirous to be confirmed" reflected the fact that so many people in the vast English dioceses were going unconfirmed. Daniel Waterland (1683–1740), perhaps the most distinguished Anglican theologian of his day, nowhere mentions Confirmation in the six published volumes of his works, judging from a very detailed index.

Yet in nineteenth-century America Confirmation became very important, again for reasons of structuring our piety. Bishop John Hobart (1775–1830) of New York saw Confirmation as a means of overcoming the congregationalism of Episcopalians in New York, and therefore went about insisting on the laying on of hands. Confirmation became the mark of being an Episcopalian. This was so true that in the 1892 revision of the Book of Common

Prayer the passage from Acts 8:14–18 was added as a means of proving that the Episcopal Church was engaged in a scriptural practice. In a land where revivalism and "believer's Baptism" was dominant, Confirmation provided a hedge against the charge that infant Baptism is irresponsible. After all, we could say, we do require that children own their faith in this ritual.

The theological link between the late ancient and medieval chrismation and the post-Reformation Confirmation does not seem to have been fully explored until the issue of the relationship of Anglicanism to the historic Catholic Church was raised in the Oxford Movement of the mid-nineteenth century. No one spoke of Cranmer's rite as imparting character, until we found it important to show that the sacramental system had been perpetuated in its full integrity from Christ until now, an "integrity" somewhat uncritically interpreted by late medieval (and early modern) Roman Catholic theology and practice. The brittle dogmatism of the nineteenth century, with its rather naive view of history, led some Anglican theologians to ignore the evidence and assume that there were no problems in adopting the whole tradition in regard to Confirmation prior to the sixteenth century and to apply it to the "bishoping" we had known in Anglicanism since 1549.* This set the stage for the debate of the last generation.

It is not difficult for some of us to recall Dom Gregory Dix's suggestion in 1946 that Baptism is only a preliminary to Confirmation, which is what makes membership in Christ operative, Dix had depended on the writings of A. J. Mason, a fellow of Trinity, Cambridge, in England,

---

* Needless to say, I am describing here the popular prevailing theology of the day and not the profound works of such notables as R. I. Wilberforce, John Henry Newman, F. D. Maurice, Samuel Taylor Coleridge, etc.

who had said that Baptism is an inchoate thing, demanding the gift of the Spirit in Confirmation. It is easy to document Mason's misuse of quotations from the Church Fathers. It took G. W. H. Lampe in 1951 to call all this into question, which he did, unfortunately overstating his case as polemicists tend to do (including perhaps myself).*
It is out of this struggle that the present attempts to understand the role of Confirmation come.

SUMMARY

The question with which I began this chapter was whether or not Confirmation, as we know it in the Episcopal Church, was not the traditional and appropriate means for the Christian to celebrate his maturity in the faith. To many people it seems so obvious. Recently I read an article by a priest in *The Christian Challenge* who said that to tamper with the service of Confirmation as inherited in the Book of Common Prayer was to violate one's ordination vows. Certainly the difficulty in maintaining that argument should be obvious now; for the Church has been tampering with the meaning and forms of Confirmation since it came to be in the political life of the Church.

In considering the basic issue relative to this study, three points can be drawn from this discussion of the Confirmation rite.

First, whatever Confirmation may denote, that which has the longest, undisturbed history in the rite is the name itself. Even at that, Confirmation is not of scriptural warrant. The matter, form, minister, and intent has varied

* L. S. Thornton contributed a book to this argument after Lampe's study in 1956. His position, as best one can tell, was a kind of tempered support of Dix. This confused study is not considered one of Thornton's better works.

to some degree. Even the importance of the rite to the recipient has been in question at various times and places.

Second, theologically the most consistent interpretation of whatever has gone under the name of Confirmation is that it *strengthens* the recipient with the Holy Spirit that he may grow in Christian faith and witness. Notions of status-change effected by the rite, such as the impartation of character would require, have been most obscure.

Third, the Church did not intend from the start that Confirmation be a maturity rite. There are hints of it in Aquinas, and clearly Cranmer so intended. However, Cranmer created something new, collapsing the old back into Baptism, and gave that new thing the minister and name of the old. His understanding of maturity was completely shaped in the sixteenth-century notions of human development.

This being true, it is not possible to argue from a single or clear tradition of Confirmation as to what the perimeters are of the ritualization of our coming of age in the Church. There are no simple givens which will speak exhaustively to the situation in which we find ourselves today. What is necessary, having looked at the situation of the committed Christian in today's world as we did in the first chapter, is for us to illuminate that situation by means of a basic theological interpretation and then to build anew the possibilities for the ritual celebration of our maturity in Christ. It is entirely appropriate to do this in terms of the inherited cluster of associations with Confirmation, but not in a way that tyrannizes the contemporary Church. It is the purpose of the next chapter to move to the theological question.

3

A theology of a maturity rite

"The Christian is then no longer so much one who possesses grace (as if it were more or less certain that this were not the case with non-Christians) but one in whom grace wishes to reveal itself in history." That is a quotation from the contemporary German Jesuit, Karl Rahner. If we keep in mind that for Rahner grace is the presence of God, then the contrast in this statement becomes even more apparent. The mature Christian is not one who owns God by owning his faith, but rather he is one who has so surrendered his life to God that he has become an instrument of God's purpose in the world.

Aquinas is quite right, then, in associating Christian maturity with our witness to the world. He who knows God perceives his vision for creation. To know God is to experience the love of God, for it is the love of God that first opens our sight to his presence. Therefore, he who perceives God's vision for creation cannot help but experience the motivating power of love to act for the fulfillment of that vision. This is what our Lord must mean when he says that the test of our faith is the fruit of our life (Mt. 7:16–20).

Where Aquinas was wrong was to identify maturity with some particular "perfect age" in the sense of a completed time when our potentialities are fulfilled. There is no point in a person's developmental cycle where we could say that now he had "arrived." Cranmer spoke of the "perfect age" as the time when a child has come to the "years of discretion." If we judge this occasion on the basis of cognitive or moral development, we know very well that all of life is a process of growth, which no chronological milestone can guarantee. Our development toward the *ideal* of maturity is a function of both our inner capacity and intent and the society with which we interact.

What I want to suggest in this chapter is that any maturity rite has to reflect the Christian life as *growth toward a maturity*. We achieve such maturity to the degree that we become instruments or servants in whom God, to quote St. Paul, "has caused his light to shine . . . to give the light of revelation—the revelation of the glory of God in the face of Jesus Christ" (II Cor. 4:6). My undergirding assumption is that the religious life is by nature a quest or search for a maturity that can only be measured in Christ. A ritualization of maturity, therefore, has somehow to be related to that quest.

As we look at the question of becoming a mature Christian—"one in whom grace wishes to reveal itself in history"—the following theological notions will be of interest. First, it is helpful to consider the age-old controversy surrounding the distinction between justification and sanctification. I am not sure whether we assume these distinctions in Anglicanism, have repudiated them, or have forgotten them. Certainly they are not much talked about. Second, outside the Church there is no salvation. As intolerant as this may seem and has been interpreted, it is true in one important sense. Third, if that is not enough,

I agree with Ignatius of Antioch (c. 35–c. 107) that the bishop represents Christ and, therefore, the universal Church.

If the reader senses that these three traditional subjects from theology make strange "bedfellows" in a book that is questioning some of our past traditions, it is understandable. I do not think that this is being inconsistent, however, because it needs to be kept in mind that the goal is to illuminate the contemporary situation, which involves both taking the past seriously and altering some of the presuppositions about the meaning of justification *versus* sanctification, the necessity of the Church, and the role of the episcopate.

BORN AND GROWING

A colleague of mine recently caused some stir where I teach when he remarked in a sermon that Baptism is the most important of the sacraments. I think he is quite correct, if for no other reason than that Baptism makes possible everything else. It is in this sense the sacrament of justification. The service in the 1928 Book of Common Prayer, immediately following the consignation reads: "Seeing now, dearly beloved brethren, this Child is regenerate, and grafted into the Body of Christ"—by virtue of what we have just done! The baptismal liturgy in the proposed rites, after the dipping and consignation, reads: "We receive you into the household of God. Confess the faith of Christ crucified, proclaim his resurrection, and share with us in his eternal priesthood." These are both formulas declaring that the candidate is now justified.

What do we mean by "justified"? The question of justification first appears in Christian theology in a significant manner in Augustine of Hippo. His personal journey from paganism to Christianity, dramatically effected in a conversion experience, culminating in an event he records in the eighth chapter of his *Confessions*, colors much of Augustine's perception of the Christian life. St. Paul, who had a similar conversion experience, is an important source for Augustine, for both share from their past a sense of the decisive nature of God's call to them. Paul speaks at length of being "counted righteous," not because of anything we have done, but only because of our faith in God's saving act. Jesus was, he says, "given up to death for our misdeeds, and raised to life to justify us" (Rom. 4:25). Augustine, using the Latin translation of the Bible, read Paul to mean that we are *made* righteous. The reformers, particularly Martin Luther, understood Paul to mean we are *imputed* righteousness or *treated as if* righteous, implying that the man who is in Christ is both justified and still in his sin.

This notion of justification certainly implies that by an absolute act of God man is the recipient of God's presence or grace in our life, by the power of Christ's death and resurrection. This is the free gift of God, which has a twofold effect. We are forgiven our sins and we are brought into a new relationship with God. This is not to say that we no longer live in terms of the effects of man's sinful state, but that we are no longer held culpable for the sin of the world and that we are in a relationship in which the presence of God has the potentiality of living and working through us to bring us to maturity.

The analogy of justification is new birth. Remember the story of Nicodemus, who comes to Jesus to see what he had to offer (Jn. 3:1–8). Jesus tells him that if he wants to see the kingdom of God, which is perhaps a way of speaking of Christian sainthood, he must be born again.

This puzzles Nicodemus, and so Jesus explains, "No one can enter the kingdom of God without being born from water and spirit" (Jn. 3:5). Here, in all probability, the evangelist has in mind a series of images: the Baptism of John the Baptist and his prediction that one would come who would baptize in the Spirit, Christian Baptism as practiced in the early Church, and the promise of the new age which the apostolic Church thought was imminent. Paul's teaching concerning justification is not something with which the evangelist is familiar, but both share the same notion of Baptism. As Paul says, "we were baptized in union with Christ Jesus. . . . By baptism we were buried with him . . . that, as Christ was raised from the dead . . . so also we might set our feet upon the new path of life" (Rom. 6:3–4). Clearly the rite of Baptism is a sacramental celebration of new birth or of justification.

If we think of justification in this sense as effected through a sacramental act, then we see that it is more than merely a judgment that we are treated as if righteous while, in fact, being sinners. The alienation between God and man, which sin both causes and signifies, has been overcome. Baptism is not merely a juridical act, it is a symbol by means of which love is shared between God and man. I agree with the more Catholic tradition that God is present in the life of the baptized, and not still existing totally apart from man.* Just as we are born into a

* The theological student might be helped by Karl Rahner's statement: "In the classical Protestant doctrine . . . justification of man is only 'juridical.' It consists in the gracious will with which God regards the sinner, but ultimately leaves him in his sinful condition. . . . Another conception is involved in this with regard to the possibility of an 'immanent' consummation [i.e., the drive toward wholeness of person proper to the resources of the person himself] in the Catholic doctrine of justification, in which grace pervades the essence of man from his very roots with divine influence, and thereby gives him the possibility of acting positively for his own salvation, and so implants in him a free and active tendency towards his own consummation."

human family and participate as an actual member of that family in terms of who we, in fact, are, so does the person whose justification is celebrated in Baptism become, in terms of who he is, a member of God's family. The potential for God is fulfilled to that extent.

However, this does not mean that one is righteous in the sense of being a perfect or complete human being. Justification is the establishment of the relationship which makes growth in Christ possible. This is why Baptism is necessary, but only marks a beginning. Next comes the whole maturing process, which continues rooted in the analogy of growing up in the family into which one has been born. This process is then related to what is traditionally meant by sanctification as the vineyard is to the vintage wine. Vatican II held that one of the three basic functions of the ordained ministry of the Church was to be an agent of sanctification, by which it meant that the clergy are to strive to enable the members of the Church to grow to that fullness of life or being for which God intended them. To do this they have to be concerned that persons mature in order that they may be fit subjects for sanctification.

In other words, there is a *dual* process, which comes under the title of hominisation, "becoming human." There is the *natural* dimension of this process of hominisation, where the inner capacities or potentialities of the person mature within the developmental cycle. It is to this I refer in speaking of the maturing process. Then there is the *graced* dimension. Sanctification is the process whereby the grace of God completes or perfects the natural self. Grace does not act contrary to the developmental cycle, but infuses the life of a person at each stage of his earthly journey to give a divine dimension to his development at that point. The end of sanctification is sainthood, which, however, requires maturity. Hominisation is the process, then, of becoming whole or of being saved, in the sense that one's created potential for God, which has been thwarted by the sin of the world, is fulfilled by the grace of God.

The hominisation process needs strength for growth. Just as little children are sometimes told, "Eat your vegetables, you need the strength to grow," so does the Church feed us that we might have the strength to grow into the full manhood of Christ (Eph. 4:13). Yet, just as children must be mature enough to acknowledge the need for a balanced diet, so must the Christian be developing the maturity to see the need for spiritual strength. The ritual events which communicate such strength are rites of intensification, rather than rites of passage from one status to another, as in Baptism. The reader needs to remember that the rites of intensification are related to the cycle of the seasons, the drawing upon the vitality of nature to insure the feeding of the participants through the progress of their life. Sanctification is a process that depends upon the celebration of such rites by maturing Christians.

In introducing the notion of rites of intensification into sacramental theology, it should be noted that the liturgical dimensions of sanctification take on a deeper and more universal dimension. Because they are related to the order of creation and not to the order of society, rites of intensification draw on the power of God's presence in nature and are obscured by the cultural filters of religion. When one participates in a rite of intensification he is better able to stand outside the issues of the civil or invisible religion, as discussed in the first chapter.

Obviously the supreme rite of intensification in the Church is the Eucharist. Its predominant image of the action of feeding, tied to the participation in the power of the Cross, immediately brings this to mind. The Sacrament of Penance might also be thought of as a rite of intensification, but actually there is a certain *passage* involved here. Penance recalls the original remission of sin, the passage from a state of sin to one of acceptance in the Church, effected by Baptism. In this sense it is much more a participation in Baptism than any kind of maturity rite.* In a certain sense it restores us to the status of our Baptism. It seems to me much more characteristic of Confirmation to be a rite of intensification than Penance, and in this sense it is second only to the Eucharist.

In saying this I am picking up the recurrent theme in medieval theology, as well as in the Book of Common Prayer, that Confirmation *strengthens* the maturing recipient in his *growth* toward sanctification. It is then a rite that does not celebrate the person's justification but rather his sanctification. It is a sacramental act involved in helping us once we "set our feet upon the new path of life."

The occasion of a maturity rite, to speak loosely of Confirmation in this sense, is different from the Eucharist. It is certainly less frequent than our participation in the Eucharist—the tradition would say only once—and its relationship to the Eucharist is clearly instrumental. By this I mean that any maturity rite would be a strengthening of a faith in which the Eucharist is the prevailing center of participation in that faith. In other words, Confirmation—to use that term—partakes of the same saving action of God in Christ as the Eucharist, but only through a different form of sacramental participation and on a different occasion in our lives.

* Without engaging in a long discourse, among others of the traditional seven sacraments I would classify Marriage and Orders as rites of passage, although I think it could be argued that Marriage is also a rite of intensification. Unction, as I suggested in the first chapter, as a healing rite does not easily fit in either category.

The saving action is Christ's passion. The Holy Spirit was at Calvary and at the tomb, and he comes to us in the Eucharist and at any other time in the power of these paschal mysteries. Once we transcend the "tour-guide mentality" of the Easter cycle of the Christian year, developed by the fourth-century Jerusalem Church, and stop thinking of Calvary, the empty tomb, the Ascension, and Pentecost as discrete events at four different places, then we can begin to think of the Holy Spirit as present and effective for us in the total, single event of our salvation: the suffering-death-resurrection-exaltation-gift of the Spirit of Jesus.* All participation in Christ is in this total event. The strengthening by the Holy Spirit in a maturity rite is not a "Pentecost event" as opposed, say, to Baptism as a participation in the "Easter event," but the power of God given to us in the total salvation event or paschal mysteries in any sacramental context. After all, it was in a *resurrection* appearance of our Lord, where "he breathed on them [his disciples], saying, 'Receive the Holy Spirit.' " (Jn. 20:22)

As I have suggested all along, a maturity rite, then, is one in which we are strengthened in our faith by the conscious affirmation of our responsibility to the Cross and Resurrection. Yet just as sanctification is not some-

* The Church in Jerusalem during the fourth century developed quite a tourist business, as evidenced in a journal we still have describing a tour: *The Pilgrimage of Etheria*, the work of probably a Spanish abbess. It was at this time that the sites of Calvary, the Resurrection, the Ascension, and Pentecost were identified and they became pilgrim shrines. Granting the difficulty of finding these sites almost 400 years later—the equivalent of discovering today where a notable bandit was buried at the end of the reign of Elizabeth I—the whole idea depends on the Lukan scenario and chronology. Whatever Luke's purposes may have been in developing the sequence of events as he did, other Gospel writers handle the same theological notion of suffering-death-resurrection-exaltation-gift of the Spirit as the saving event in a different manner. This is particularly true of the fourth Gospel.

thing which goes on within an individual, but is always relational—for sanctification has to do with becoming what we are, and to *be* is to *be in relation*—so the owning of our faith in the paschal mysteries is always related to our relationship to the community of faith, the community of the Resurrection. In fact, I would argue that a ritualization of our taking responsibility for our faith is not only done within the context of the community, but is performed in terms of our perception of ourselves in relationship to that community. This is the subject of the next section.

THE QUEST FOR COMMUNITY

Arthur Vogel, Bishop of the Episcopal Diocese of West Missouri and a distinguished theologian, has written, "Persons can be themselves only with other persons, which means that absolute difference, not relative difference, is constitutive of personal being. . . . Intensity of distinction is the source of richness in personal relationships." This is a puzzling and profound statement, a commentary on what Vogel means when he says that a person does not *have* a community, he *is* his community. This is not to say that the individual counts for nothing, as Vogel makes clear, but that without the extension of our person beyond our body into the community of which we are a part we would not be an individual. To become human it is necessary to be a member of a community which is humanizing.

It is a generally accepted axiom in the anthropology of religion that religion consists of three constants: community, creed, and cult. The Church is, of course, the Christian community. If Christ is the norm, as I believe he is, for being human, as well as the source of the power to achieve that end, then his community is essential to that process. Jesus' death and resurrection is the event that calls the community into being, for it is the means for making the power of that event effective in the life of man. This is a kind of logic not always guaranteed to encourage agreement, because some of us have felt that the Church as we have experienced it is anything but humanizing. Yet, be that as it may, it is true, no matter what our experience, that we cannot become alone that person "in whom grace wishes to reveal itself" (to cite Rahner again). This is why I would insist that the ancient axiom, "Outside the Church there is no salvation," is true.

But that is to say nothing more than that God's sanctifying presence and the experience of hominisation takes place necessarily in community. It is not to identify the Church with one entity—such as the Anglican Communion, the Reformed tradition, or the Holy Roman Church—as opposed to another. I am not suggesting either that the Church is "as wide as the love of God," as I once heard a well-intended preacher say. Certainly Hans Küng, the German Roman Catholic theologian, is correct when he suggests in his book, *The Church*, that a combination of the four creedal signs of the Church (one, holy, Catholic, and apostolic) with the Protestant signs ("where the Gospel is taught in its purity and the sacraments properly ministered") provides a basic criterion for what we mean by the dimensions of the Lord's community.* But this sets before us an ideal, a canon more than anything else, by which we can judge how far short our concrete community falls.

* It is not my intention to pursue a discussion of what Küng says in this book. For those who are interested, I have particular reference to Hans Küng, *The Church*, trans. by Ray and Rosaleen Ockenden (Sheed and Ward, 1967), pp. 261–359.

It is also true that the Church as we experience it today is a pilgrim community, not an eschatological reality. It is not the kingdom of God. It is broken, fallible, sinful, and confused. If we can believe that God works through this community we know that he can raise to life the dead bones of men. To experience the Church is to know frustration and disillusionment, but it is also to know the miracle of life amid death. I never cease to be amazed at the vitality of the Christian community, to which I must confess I owe what I am at my best. Often we are blind to the amazing way that the love of God still seems to flow through even the worst expressions of the Body of Christ.

The fact that there is no wholeness of a person in Christ outside of the redeeming community of our Lord, coupled with the obvious blindness and inhumanity of the Church, compels me to dwell a little further on this seeming incongruity. It also provides the basis for what I want to say about the relationship of the process of sanctification, its ritualization, and the Church. But first, Daniel Day Williams, a scholar and theologian at Union Theological Seminary in New York until his recent death, once wrote: "Let us describe the Church as the community which lives by participation in the atonement." This statement is an important clue to living with an all-too-human Church. The atonement is the effect of the Cross, as we know, and it follows that to participate in the Cross of Jesus is to know all the contradiction that is focused in that event of Good Friday. It is, among other things, the religious establishment—the Church of the Old Covenant—that crucified Jesus, and it is the rudiments of the Church of the New Covenant that fled from Calvary in terror.

Simone Weil (1909–1943) was a French Jew who fought in the resistance movement and whose best known writings, published under the title *Waiting for God*, are considered one of the great classics of Christian spirituality of this century.* I mention her here because she loved our Lord and yet never became a member of the Church, for reasons which relate to the problem discussed here. Having experienced the horrors of the German invasion of France, she was very suspicious of what she called "social enthusiasms," including the joy—the triumphalism, if you will—derived from knowing one is a member of the Mystical Body of Christ. Every collectivism, she believed, is given to the abuse of power and can lead to the horror of totalitarianism. She goes on to say: "I think it is as well that a few sheep should remain outside the fold in order to bear witness that the love of Christ is essentially something different" than social enthusiasm.

It is, but the anomaly is that even Simone Weil had to have the Church to tell her about such love. The priest, the Gospels, and the Eucharist which told her the story of God in Jesus are all of the Church, despite her suggestion to the contrary. If she bore witness in faith to Christ until death, as she undoubtedly did, it was because the Church made it possible, this same Church which committed the horror of the Inquisition and still today remains so often impervious to obvious truth.

Having said this, it seems to me that the spiritual quest of the aware Christian is for a kind of unhappy marriage with the Church. Perhaps the reader remembers the story of the Easterner who comes into town in the old West and goes into a saloon to watch roulette. As he stands there he can see that the game is blatantly dishonest. He asks one poor soul, who has been losing all night long, "Why are you playing here? Don't you see the wheel is crooked?"

* This work is published in English under the title of *Waiting for God.* I prefer a different preposition, *Waiting on God,* which more accurately reflects the spirit of the Greek phrase on which the title is based, *en hupomenē.*

"Of course," comes the reply, "but it's the only game in town." The Church is the only game in town where one can experience the Gospel.

Like many tumultuous marriages, however, the spiritual quest has to be renegotiated time and time again. For one reason, we are never quite sure of our partner. We live in a very mobile society. Anyone who has moved around, as most of us have, is aware that congregations of Christians vary in astounding ways from place to place. Certainly, as organizational development has shown us, there are certain constants to the dynamics of parish life.* Yet even a denominational name, such as "Episcopal," will not guarantee the newcomer what he may expect when he enters the Church doors. Change is characteristic of Church life, and every congregation changes in its own unique way, just as every one of us changes. The maturing process and the life of the spirit come together in the Christian community, but that community is not static or unchanging as we move through life, anymore than we are the same person now as we were five or ten years ago. This means that our responsibility to our faith, within the process of sanctification, faces a challenge whenever we become acutely aware of the change in the Christian congregation of which we are a part. It faces an even greater challenge when we become aware of the inevitable change within us, which is a second reason for constant renegotiation of our marriage to the Church.

In 1966 I moved from Louisiana to Wisconsin. In 1973 I returned south to Tennessee. One of my friends from Louisiana days remarked with some amazement when he

* Loren Mead and his associates point out in *New Hope for Congregations* (Seabury, 1972), that congregations are interpersonal systems and have the general characteristics of such. However, one of those characteristics is that each system is unique. "No two congregations are alike," says Mead.

met me again in Tennessee that I was not the same person he had known seven or eight years before. My honest reply was: "I surely hope not!" The only people who remain the same are dead. Furthermore, the Church I knew in Louisiana is not the same Church I knew in Wisconsin and now experience in Tennessee, but it does no good to lament this fact. Different as I am, I have to work out my faith commitment in terms of the Church I know now. Nostalgia is, as Bonhoeffer once wrote, a "death leap."

There is no doubt that there are critical times—in the sense of turning points—when we need to take a look once again at one's relationship to the Church and to ritualize that further step in the process of maturing within the context of the redeeming community. This may be only once in our life, but in our culture it is much more likely to be three or four times over a period of forty or fifty years. There are the times we move or the rector or vicar moves. There are occasions when a divorce or a death in our immediate family calls our faith into question. The loss of a job, the discovery of or recovery from a serious illness, a sudden success, a return from a dangerous assignment, all might evoke in us a need to ritualize again our owning of our faith. (How much better it would be for someone returning from war to do this rather than feel he had to enter the priesthood.) There is also the simple, slow erosion of our enthusiasm, which study and reaffirmation can seek to reverse.

I know that some would say that now I am referring to rites of reaffirmation and they would insist that Confirmation is different. How is this so? The traditional argument, once it got outside the circular logic that Confirmation is an unrepeatable something because we have never re-peated it, is to say that it imparts character. I have no objection to the notion of character in the sense that Karl

Rahner defines it. For him character is that which gives a person

once and for all a very definite, permanent assimilation to Christ and a social connection with him as head of the Church, and hence *assign[s] him a place in the social organism of the Church* [emphasis added].

I think Baptism and Ordination do this. I hope I have made it reasonably clear in the first chapter that Confirmation does not.

A more recent argument for the separation of Confirmation from any notion of reaffirmation is to say that when one makes an *initial* affirmation of his baptismal vows in the maturing process, this is such a momentous occasion that it must be set apart in matter, form, and possibly minister to keep from cheapening it. I call this the argument from subjective intentionality. It is fraught with all kinds of problems.

On the level of personal experience and practice, it is simply untrue. My two middle children were confirmed at age nine. Both of them have testified to me that this was a meaningless experience and that they would very much like to have the opportunity to repeat it. There are other variables (age, freedom of choice, significant others, general outlook, etc.) than the matter of being the "first," which influence the subjective impact of a significant act. Our first confession, our first Communion, our first experience of sexual intercourse, our first child's birth can all be very significant experiences unlike any other. However, in those four examples I have listed, I am sure that I have mentioned at least one which, to the adult reader, was either a matter of indifference or sheer disaster on the first occasion. Furthermore, I do not think that subsequent confessions, communions, coital acts, or acts of parturition cheapened any initial "high" we may recall.

On a more theoretical level, the argument from subjective intentionality commits the basic sociological error that we can know the subjective intention of another or even control it. The great German sociologist, Max Weber (1864–1920), devoted his life to the understanding of the subjective intention of others and failed. Such things as emotional investment in the other and the value-sets of the subject are not available to our observation or control. Therefore, there is no data to support the notion that a first affirmation, even if set at the supposed ideal age (which I shall discuss in the next chapter), is so significant that it must be ritually set apart from every subsequent reaffirmation; nor is there any way that we can control it so that it will be. The insistence that we must distinguish between Confirmation and subsequent reaffirmation is more the result of our own inherited tradition coloring our thought than anything that can be supported by the data.

I will return to this subject in the next chapter. The purpose here has been to state the relation of maturity rites in the process of hominisation to the Christian community. I have said that the "marriage" to the Church is essential for the fulfillment of that process, but that it will be in our society a tumultuous relationship to most people. In shaping any maturity rite, we must take both of these factors into consideration. I will leave the patterning of the rite to the fourth chapter, but it is important to say something further here about the relationship of the rite to the community.

THE NECESSITY OF THE EPISCOPATE

Every particular Christian community is a microcosm of the Catholic or universal Church. The universal Church is, on the other hand, not limited by a moment in history or a particular place. It possesses a continuity of time and space, which a given congregation does not. When God entered the world in the birth, life, death, and resurrection of Jesus, he did so in terms of a particular moment and place in history. That event, however, was proleptic of the entire sweep of history, and it would be an error to think of the Incarnation in terms of a first-century Palestinian culture without a transcending truth to be fulfilled at the end of history.*

I am sure that this appears to be a very abstract concept, even if we agree with it. The given congregation of which we are a part is concrete. The talk of "continuity," "prolepsis," and the "end of history" is not. The task of the bishop, as I see it, is to give substance to the notion of continuity and what that implies in terms of the relation of the Christ event to history. Since the Church, as I have suggested, is a pilgrim community, it is a people going somewhere. That "somewhere" is the vision given in the life of our Lord, and the power to make this journey is found in the mystery of his death and resurrection. The episcopate is the abiding sign of the integrity of the continuing quest, as it is related to Christ's saving action and example.

The proposed ordinal speaks of the bishop as the "guardian of the Church's faith." The tendency is to think of "the Church's faith" as *notional.* By this I mean faith as the answer to the question: "What do you believe?" While I have no intention of dismissing the importance of knowing what you believe, I have more in mind what is

* The word "proleptic" refers here to the belief that the life of Jesus anticipated the character of human existence at the end of history and therefore is a concrete manifestation of the goal of hominisation. Wolfhart Pannenberg, a German theologian, is the principal exponent of this Christological stance.

often called *real* faith. By this I mean *the trust in the promises of God* revealed to us in the history of the Hebrew people and, particularly, in Christ. By this I also mean an awareness of the truth that amid all the relativism of our culture there is a Power that undergirds the very existence of the self even in the midst of despair, even as Christ cried out upon the Cross. To guard such a faith is not so much to conduct heresy trials as it is to live in continuity with Jesus and that community which embodies his trust and awareness, and to signify both the hope and judgment for our lives given in this Gospel.

The bishop is, therefore, one who always embodies a transcendence of the immediate. One of the selections suggested for the epistle at the ordination of a bishop speaks of the high priesthood of Christ, which presumably the bishop is to use as a pattern. It reads in part, "He [Jesus] learned obedience in the school of suffering and, once perfected, became the source of eternal salvation for all who obey him" (Heb. 5:8–10). Behind this passage there is the obvious commitment to the belief that one who serves more than this passing age will suffer, and ought to suffer, but out of that comes the wholeness that God would give. The episcopate, therefore, becomes the expression of that refusal of the pilgrim community to see everything in terms of the present and also the expression of the demand of the Gospel that we take the present with great seriousness for the sake of the future.

Sometimes I think the Eastern Orthodox have a point in not having married bishops. It is difficult to combine the married and episcopal vocations. Certainly the episcopate would greatly profit if it would pattern its membership upon the *starets*, the Russian holy man, long on the experience of the spiritual life. For the authority of the episcopate cannot be said to be contained in the canonical structures of the Church. Whereas arguments from tactual successions of bishops can have a symbolic value, in the end they guarantee nothing. The authority of the episcopate has to come from the inherited wisdom and the pastoral tradition of the office, as well as from the personal holiness of him who is called. It is the authority of love, which the New Testament describes as the authority of Christ.

It is very important that one who wishes to affirm his relationship to the Christian community, effected at his Baptism, not only do it in terms of the concrete community of which he is a part, but in the clear symbolization of the Catholic Church of which that given congregation is an expression. This is why, it seems to me, the bishop is the essential minister of all maturity rites. In the process of the given individual's hominisation, he is participating in the hominisation of the world. His personal pilgrimage must, therefore, be related to the pilgrimage of the people of God as a whole, unbounded by time or place. The fact that he comes to the bishop for the laying on of hands ties what he intends into the everlasting vocation of the entire people of God. There is a dialectic of the particular and the concrete represented in the given congregation in that moment and place with the life of the universal Church that transcends any discrete expression as signified in the bishop.

I am not arguing here for the dominical institution of the monarchial episcopate. Neither am I seeking to "un-Church" those who have, in centuries past, abrogated the episcopate.* I am saying that for the Episcopal

* Carl Braaten, an eminent Lutheran theologian, writes: "There has never existed a human community that could survive without leadership. It is no different in the Christian community. Whether Christ instituted a special ministry of leadership in the church or not, it was bound to arise. But such a

Church, as well as other communions, the episcopate is the historic sign of the transcendent vocation of the Church. The image from the ancient Church of the penitent kneeling before the bishop to receive the laying on of hands and to be reconciled once again to community of hope is very much in my mind. I am also thinking of such witnesses as Cyprian (d. 258), who, rather than flee persecution, finally died a martyr in his diocese; and Samuel Isaac Joseph Schereschewsky (1831–1906), who served his diocese for twenty years by translating the Holy Scriptures for them while almost completely paralyzed. In the presence of such a history one can affirm with Ignatius, himself on the way to a martyr's death, "Wherever the bishop appears, let the people be, just as wherever Christ is, there is the universal church." * For in suffering they have embodied the obedience to God's vision for us, and show forth the authority of Christ's love. Somehow this image of the bishop overcomes the humanity of bishops, as well as of the rest of us. This image of the bishop also lays before us a clear sign of the continuing pilgrimage in which the people of God partake as the context of their maturing in Christ.

What I am pleading for is the sense of a very personal relationship between the bishop and his people, which the rites of maturity would constantly reinforce. For this

---

ministry is not autonomous. . . . The succession of ordained officeholders, transmitted in an episcopal sense, is actually a sign of the continuity of the whole church with its apostolic origins. It is a *sign* and not the *reality* itself. . . . It is a highly desirable sign, because it symbolizes the apostolicity of the church in a specially vivid way."

* This appears in Ignatius's letter to the Smyrnaeans. Apparently the development of the monarchial episcopate was much more rapid in Syria and Asia Minor than elsewhere. Ignatius had a very metaphorical mind. He equates the bishop to God and the presbyters to the apostles. The deacons are "entrusted with the service of Christ."

reason I think it would be wrong to make some arbitrary division between the first occasion for such a rite and all subsequent acts. It would defeat the very thing we deserve: a close association between the individual's quest to become a vessel of God's grace and the vocation of the Catholic Church to be the community of grace. What we are talking about is sanctification, and the bishop particularly has the vocation, if Vatican II is correct, of being an instrument of sanctification for the people of God.

SUMMARY

I grew up with the idea of a Christian who had "arrived," so to speak, as someone lolling around in Heaven looking at God forever. It was a very static, passive, and boring notion. I began this chapter by quoting Rahner, who gives us a very active, dynamic, and exciting (if threatening) image: "The Christian is . . . one in whom grace wishes to reveal itself in history." The rest of what I have said has sought to show how maturity rites fit into enabling us to achieve that much more desirable goal. Among the points I have made are the following:

First, once we are justified we are always justified, and Baptism celebrates this new relationship with God. The rest of the process of becoming that to which we are called by God to be is sanctification, and maturity rites are very much a part of this struggle to be responsive to God's call. In saying this I have picked up on the traditional language of strength and growth, as effected through the laying on of hands, without attempting to claim any particular passage in status or identification of an age of maturity.

Second, growth in Christ is always growth by means of the Body of Christ, the Church. We cannot become ourselves apart from the redeeming community. This is in spite of the sin of the world which is so often evident in the Church. Therefore, a maturity rite is one of finding ourselves within the Church, something that we might logically expect could be desirable more than once in a long lifetime.

Third, the proper minister of such a rite is the bishop. The symbolic reality of the episcopate is that of the continuity in time and place of the Church. The owning of one's faith, that necessarily and appropriately takes place in terms of a unique, concrete congregation, needs the contrapuntal dimension of the relationship to the Church which transcends the immediate incarnation of the Christ.

Fourth, there is every reason why, therefore, a maturity rite should be a normative part of the life of the Christian as he develops in his faith. There is no theological reason why that rite must never be repeated, and good reasons why we might expect that to happen.

The first chapter looked at the value of owning one's faith in the light of our contemporary cultural situation. A certain ambiguity between this need and the norm of a transcultural conversion in the early Church was noted, and I suggested that we might keep this tension always in mind. However, having granted this, it was suggested that Baptism is the Christian rite of passage, and that any responsibility we might take for our baptismal vows would more appropriately be ritualized in the light of a person's developmental cycle as a rite of intensification.

In the second chapter we looked at the history of what has been called "Confirmation" and saw a number of things falling under that nomenclature. In general it seems that there is no "given" in Christian practice related to this sacramental action, but that there is a growing sense of the rite as one of strengthening by the Holy Spirit of a person in the maturing process. This notion needs, however, to be seen in a contemporary context.

This chapter now concluded has sought to spell out what that may mean theologically. The need now is to move on to what that implies in terms of practice. Theology does not always tell us what to do, but it does set the perimeters within which our doing as a Christian community is in accord with our understanding of God's relationship to his world.

4

Coming of age
in the church

One way of distinguishing between a conservative and a liberal would be to say that the former is one who holds to tradition unless he has a very good reason for changing, and the latter is one who avoids tradition unless he has a very good reason for remaining in it. While labels do as much as anything else to obscure the truth about people, I suppose that under this definition I would be more a conservative than a liberal. I think it is more realistic. Tradition means what has been "handed down" or "given over," and there is an inevitable refinement in this process. The end product, the inherited tradition, often carries a depth and universality which illuminates the meaning of our experience and leads us further into the richness of human existence than the appealing novelty or the latest fad. There can be problems, however, in being too ready to follow the tradition.

In the first place, tradition is not infallible. It can be the crystallization of something from the past, which is the result of a misplaced veneration. For example, the Gothic revival, which was part of the Romantic movement of the last century, patterned church architecture not after the medieval parish church but the medieval cathedral. Such cathedrals were built more as expressions of the piety of the day—and it was a great day—and as centers for religious communities than as places of regular Sunday worship. The choir was, of course, where the monks gathered for the daily office, and the chief seat, called the "cathedra" or "chair," was the bishop's throne. The rood screen divided the cloistered worship of the religious community from all the other activities that might go on in the nave, such as county fairs, drama, and conversation. Now in the nineteenth century, in imitations in each diocese across the land, we had dozens of "cathedrals." Vested choristers sat in the choir, which was the worst place possible, musically. The altar was obscured for the worshipers by their presence, if not already hidden by an impenetrable rood screen. We reverenced an especially uncomfortable piece of furniture and called it the bishop's chair, even though he sat in it for maybe ten minutes a year. All of this nonsense was in the name of maintaining the tradition of the Church.

Second, tradition is not always appropriate. It can be the silly solemnization of expedience. I am reminded of the story of a parish where for some years they used an illicit missal in which the canon of the Mass—the prayer of consecration—was *not* printed on two opposing pages, as it is in the Book of Common Prayer. Rather than sully his hands by turning the pages during this solemn moment, the priest had an acolyte come up and turn the page at the appropriate time. Then the parish bought a new illicit missal, in which a better job had been done. The canon was on opposing pages. The tradition was established, however, and instead of having the acolyte stay where he was during the consecration, he now came from his place to the missal, but only touched the book and returned.

Third, tradition is not stable. Whereas in one age it can represent something very appropriate and meaningful to our life, in another age it can become a source of tyranny. For example, in the early Middle Ages the collapse of the Roman Empire in the West created a havoc in which the tribal system of the Germanic peoples did little but feed fuel to the fires of chaos. Almost alone, the unquestioned authority of the Christian bishops and their appeal to reason and learning salvaged civilization. In later centuries this authority became a humanizing force amid the constant fighting between the feudal lords. In still later centuries, however, it became the tradition which opposed new learning and supported the Inquisition. It was this same authority of the episcopate in the last century which gravely injured the Church by opposing biblical criticism, the human sciences, the rights of the working man, and social change. A civilizing tradition hung on to enslave the minds of men.

We must avoid being victimized by tradition, just as we must not become the captives of our feelings. We have to gain some distance on them by asking questions of them. Tradition does not give premises by which we judge all of life. It is the source of a kind of data which may illuminate the contemporary experience in such a way that our life becomes richer and our true end is more nearly realized: our freedom to become that which we are in God's eyes. Tradition should then encourage love, beget justice, and promote reconciliation—in that order. We need to ask of tradition, therefore, the kind of questions whose answers will tell us whether it does enrich our life that we might better help the free sons and daughters of God.

Gaining distance on traditions requires a differentiation of thinking. We cannot confuse the immediate, the concrete, the particular inheritance from the past with what *is*. We have to ask ourselves in what way a given tradition explains our experience. An example relevant to this today is found in looking at maturity rites in the light of our Confirmation tradition and the contemporary experience of culture. We need to ask whether what we have been doing provides the best way of sacramentally enabling the freedom of the maturing Christian. My answer has been generally in the negative, if not unequivocally so.

A negative, even an equivocal one, is not enough. We have to offer something in its place, which takes tradition, the contemporary data, and reason with equal seriousness. The final task of this study is, therefore, to picture what might happen should the results of the previous discussion be implemented in the life of the Church. My assumption is that the reader is willing to accept with me, at least for the moment, a position of tempered conservatism and differentiated thought, and to imagine what it might mean to act responsibly. Let us sketch a picture of the ritualization of coming of age in the Church from the viewpoint, first, of the person himself; second, the parish; and, third, the bishop.

THE PERSON IN HIS RELIGIOUS DEVELOPMENT

John Westerhoff of Duke University has suggested that there is a developmental cycle in the religious life of the individual, just as there is the psycho-social, cognitive, and moral development, described by Erik Erikson, Jean Piaget, and Lawrence Kohlberg, respectively. This is to say that there are turning points in every person's growth, when certain needs have to be met, and when they are satisfied, that person acquires a new strength of self. Whenever one of these critical stages is not resolved, however, a person becomes fixed there emotionally, cognitively, morally, or religiously. He may appear to have moved on in his development, but under stress he will regress to that level of behavior and intentionality at which he became fixed.

Westerhoff wants us to understand that his thesis is tentative. It does provide, however, a basis upon which to consider the relationship of the ritualization of the maturing process to the age of the individual, as well as the context within which a person might seek to set his coming of age in the Church. There are in this system six epigenetic stages of religious development. They are the foundational (ages 0–3), the imitative (ages 3–6), the affiliative (ages 6–12), the individuating (ages 12–18), the consolidative (ages 18–25), and the universalizing (ages 25 up). Westerhoff places much emphasis, as I do, upon the role of ritual in the community of faith; and therefore he suggests that a rite of passage should effect the transition between each stage. Before the foundational stage there is a parenting rite; before the imitative, Baptism; before the affiliative, first Communion; before the individuating, covenanting (to struggle within the Church); before the consolidative, confirmation or recovenanting; and before the universalizing, there is reaffirmation.

Westerhoff goes on to say that there is also an appropriate form of the community of faith for each stage, which provides a setting for healthy interaction and growth. For the foundational stage there are the social parents; for the imitative, the generation of grandparents on a one-to-one basis; for the affiliative, an affective belonging to the congregation; for the individuating, a chance to experiment within the Church; for the consolidative, action-reflection groups with a support community; and for the universalizing, an identification in the world with the hurt, injured, and oppressed.

Criticism of this theory would be out of order at this time. As a matter of fact, I find much of it helpful and in accord with my own experience. Dialogue with Westerhoff seems to me quite appropriate, however, for I would hope to sharpen by this means my own understanding of a person's quest for maturity in Christ.

Westerhoff speaks of six developmental stages culminating in a secure, mature faith, exhibited by a sense of love, justice, and reconciliation. Karl Rahner is referring to the same thing when he speaks of "one in whom grace wishes to reveal itself in history." Certainly one does not arrive at this point at twenty-five. Westerhoff mentions that a reaffirmation rite might be repeated every five years, which is indicative of the constant struggle in the average person of faith—not to mention the religious retardates that populate our land. As a matter of judgment, it seems that the struggle of each stage is sublated into the higher stage, starting with the development of faith at the foundational level. By "sublated" I mean that the previous stage is caught up into the next stage and lived through again in terms of the higher stage.

It is evident from my discussion in the third chapter that I share Westerhoff's high doctrine of the Church. Although perhaps I only lack sufficient data, I am not able to play as loose with sacramental theology as he. He seems correct in his evaluation of first Communion, although I might place it a little earlier than he does. I am not sure what he understands a parenting or covenanting rite to effect. And I am mystified as to what he understands to be the function of Baptism. My understanding of this sacrament does not appropriately place it among six "rites of passage" along the way. It stands alone. Furthermore, whereas Westerhoff lists confirmation, re-covenanting, and reaffirmation as three distinct rites, they are in fact two dimensions of the same rite: the maturing Christian's attempt to own his faith in the face of what he knows is a never-ending struggle.

We must be careful not to let things fall out in too neat a pattern. First of all, it is questionable whether movement between psychological stages, even if they are capable of clear diagnosis (which I doubt), is appropriately assigned a rite of passage. This is to "mix apples and oranges." A rite of passage is a social phenomenon, not a psychological or physical one. Second, a rite which is repeated, as Westerhoff suggests for re-covenanting and reaffirmation, cannot be a rite of passage by definition. Third, first Communion is an important but not unique participation in a rite of intensification: the Eucharist.

The great value, for my purposes, in what Westerhoff offers in this scheme is both the movement from external to internalized faith that he identifies in the maturing process of the Christian, as well as the accompanying ability he describes of that person to witness to the grace of God in an ever more profound manner in the broadening world surrounding him. As it appears, the individual can never rest content with the nature of his interaction in the Church and, increasingly, beyond the community of faith. The Church is for the would-be saint an arena in which he tests, learns, and celebrates his growth into the manhood of Christ. The Church is also the arena for him in which he, in himself, becomes more and more the person that God in Christ would have him to be.

What I am suggesting is a pattern in this process of a tension between resolution and growing restlessness—like that of which Augustine of Hippo wrote: "My heart is restless, Lord, until it rests in you."—of an intensity varying within individuals. It is a struggle that is common, however, to all persons in our culture, as I shared in the third section of the first chapter. What we celebrate in a maturity rite is both the resolution and the certainty that we need the strength of God to live through the coming restlessness. This may happen only once in a person's life. If we want to call the initial occasion "Confirmation," I suppose there is no urgent reason why not (although I agree with the chairpersons of the diocesan liturgical commissions of the Episcopal Church who said with only one dissenting vote in a meeting in the fall of 1974 that this was only confusing). What is in error is the artificial attempt to make some binding distinction between the first celebration of a maturity rite and any possible subsequent celebrations in terms of form, matter, intention, minister, or subject. This is because a maturity rite is always basically the same for a person: a time when he celebrates a new awareness of faith within the life of the community of faith, and at the same time acknowledges his need for God's strengthening grace to grow further in his belief.

It is important to make this crisis of faith as concrete as possible. Some illustrations of such occasions, when someone would appropriately seek to ritualize his responsibility to his baptismal vows in a maturity rite, would be helpful.

I have already referred to my older son, who was confirmed at the age of ten. (My younger son is thirteen, has not been "confirmed" and has expressed no interest in it.) My older son is now nineteen, and a great deal has transpired in those nine years. The last few years have been the occasion of a classical adolescent identity struggle, including a period in the Jesus movement, along with a search for self in athletics and other typical patterns of teen-age socialization. He had a senior year in high school away from his parents that precipitated some of the anomie that characterizes so many young men their first year away from home, generally as freshmen in college. He is now a freshman, but is showing signs of behaving like a post-freshman. He is beginning to crystallize some values and the goals they establish for him. In a recent remark to me he said, "I wish there was some way, once I get it together a little better, I could have a course in religion and make some kind of commitment." His Confirmation was meaningless to him—despite any theories we might have of *ex opere operato*—and it does no good for me to say, "think about what it means to be confirmed." *

My son's situation illustrates for me some question I have with Westerhoff's contention that Confirmation should come at the end of senior high school.** As a university chaplain for ten years my experience was that the first time a person might be ready to affirm his faith in a mature manner, which includes some kind of theology, value system, and goal-setting, is at the end of his second year in college, at about age twenty. This is shortly after they begin to wonder why they joined a fraternity and have changed their major from what their father suggested to that in which they have some personal interest.***

* *Ex opere operato* means "by the work worked," and is a formula in sacramental theology which states that despite the feelings, merits, or disposition of the minister or recipient of a sacrament, divine power is imparted. As a technical term it dates from Peter of Poitiers (d. 1205). Aquinas used it in his earlier writings but apparently saw some of the problems implicit in the notion, perhaps because it implies that grace is irresistible, and therefore did not use this phrase in his later writings.

** John Wesley Stewart in his book, *Adolescent Religion*, advocated Confirmation at either fourteen or eighteen, with a preference for the former. Certainly Westerhoff is right in suggesting that fourteen makes no real sense.

*** I am writing as if the transition from high school to college is normative, and, of course, that is not true. Many persons never go to college. I can only

Another illustration of readiness of the ritualization of maturity that comes to my mind is in the case of a priest who has shared with me reflections on his coming of age. He was reared as a Southern Baptist, found the Episcopal Church as a college student, and experienced Confirmation as the climactic act of an adult quest. He never questioned the validity of his Baptism as a Baptist; but, as he has told me, the catechetical group in the Episcopal Church with which he was associated and the actual rite of Confirmation is something in terms of which he will always see the rest of his Christian life. There is no question of him seeking a repetition of the rite, but his own experience is a clear expression of the significance of the ritualization of a subjective crisis in the maturing process.

Then there is the story of John Rathbone Oliver, who was an early American pioneer in psychiatry. Oliver was brought up in the Episcopal Church, baptized and confirmed, and then wandered away. He told his personal story of his return to the Church. For a time he had felt despondent and disenchanted. Then one day he was walking along a street and saw the open door of an Episcopal church, with a sign placed at the entrance: "Confessions Now Being Heard." Suddenly he found himself drawn headlong into the church, and he almost fell into the confessional and sobbed: "I want to come home." It seems altogether fitting that there be some way beyond merely the Sacrament of Penance for someone like Oliver, who had wrestled with himself and his faith, to affirm once again his commitment to the Christian community.

While a college chaplain I came to know a student—an

speak of what I personally know, however, and that is how the vast majority of persons move—from high school to college. I will have to depend on someone with a different experience to apply what I am saying to those who move from high school to gainful employment.

Easter and Christmas Episcopalian—who truly was one of the most lovely girls I met in my ten years at Louisiana State University in Baton Rouge. That is saying a great deal. She was just about as carefree as she was beautiful. A wonderful dancer and a potential cheerleader at LSU, she was looking forward to her debut when she was gravely injured in an automobile accident. She went through the windshield of her date's car and was badly torn up. I remember our struggle together as she faced the fact that her injuries had greatly handicapped that on which she depended most: good looks and athletic ability. She proved to be a much deeper person than I had judged her to be, and she found her faith for the first time. She wanted to be rebaptized and, of course, I said no. She then asked to be reconfirmed, which request seemed to me to make sense, but again I had to say no. Why?

Also while I was at LSU there was the typical case of Fleur and Bob. She was a Roman Catholic and he was a Southern Baptist. They married and they came to the Episcopal Church in their search for a common faith. They took instruction and said they wanted to be a part of this communion. I was delighted; but when I explained that Bob would be confirmed and Fleur received, she was very angry. "What I am doing is no different than what Bob is doing, and I want to be confirmed," she insisted. "We have come to the same decision together and the fact that a bishop 'oiled' me and 'slapped' me years ago and not Bob makes no difference." I think she was right, particularly if we see the importance of subjective intentionality in maturity rites.

Monica Furlong, an English writer in spirituality, has written of the personal agony of the religious pilgrimage. "Feeling his way painfully by symbols . . . he [the contemporary pilgrim] stumbles towards unity, the unity of wholeness." I thought about this and our feelings at those times when we come to these turning points of faith and seek to give them ritual expression. I was reminded of the story in Mark's Gospel of the epileptic boy. The father desperately wanted his son to be healed, and Jesus' disciples could do nothing. He knew the power of salvation must be there, he was ready, and yet it all seemed so difficult. Even more overwrought, he came to Jesus himself and pleaded for healing for his son. Jesus replied that everything is possible for him who has faith. "I have faith," the father cried, "help me where faith falls short" (Mk. 9:24).

Every man of faith is that anxious father. Such is the crisis where a person is ready to ritualize his faith, and such is the inevitable ambiguity when he does so. The Church needs to take this with the utmost seriousness.

A PLACE TO STRUGGLE

Since coming to my present post I have no specific parish duties, so my family and I move about a good bit among various congregations of the Episcopal Church. We find them on the whole boring, with certain very notable exceptions. The problem may be ours, but in all honesty I do not believe it is. My two older children generally do not go to church when they are away, and I think they are sincere when they say the reason is that what they see in most parishes is an "in group" doing indifferent things poorly.

On reflecting on why I am bored, several things occur to me. Our options for liturgical style seem to fluctuate between self-conscious casualness toward the latest fads and a studied anachronism (as in the Society for the Preservation of the Book of Common Prayer). There is little sense of presence, of the dramatic, of the use of space and movement. We are afraid of being frightened, and the experience of God has to be frightening. Sermons are not taken seriously, despite the fact that there is strong evidence that this is the highest expectation of the average layman. When clergy are challenged in this regard I find they offer the same lame excuses for the lack of preparation or thought about what they have been doing for at least a generation. My suspicion is that if God became manifest at the average parish gathering we would all be extremely surprised. No wonder there is more religious striving being done outside the Church than in!

I sense a kind of banal humanitarianism in the Church, which adds to the boredom. We all know and use the approved language of the "third school of psychology" (as in Abraham Maslow, Gordon Allport, Carl Rogers). We have not yet advanced to the transpersonal or "fourth school." We speak of "community," "authentic lives," "self-knowledge," "communication," "openness," *ad nauseam*, without facing the suffering these things require at an honest level. It is a little difficult to find where various programs of the local mental health center leave off and the Church takes up. Our involvement in mental health is good, but by itself it is peripheral. The Church's primary concern is the experience of the mystery of God and its direct implications for the concrete values of personal daily life. I have already said in the first chapter that healthy ritual makes a great difference in how I live. I just do not see that connection being made in our parishes.

It was a president of Harvard University some years ago who said that an educated man should have developed a coherent ethical system for himself by age twenty-one and a clear philosophy of life by age thirty-five. That is a part of maturing. A parish needs to be a place where that kind of maturing and its ritualization occurs. This means that we combine liturgy—Word and Sacrament—with being a "community of moral discourse" (to use the phrase of James Gustafson of the University of Chicago).

If I were a parish priest—and I am writing as one responsible for training parish priests—I would ask myself what I was doing in my total ministry to assist the people I served to have some awareness of the issues and points of view in certain value-laden areas. I would look at the liturgy to see how it taps the power of God as experienced in a sublime feeling and focuses its meaning on God's concern for the human condition. Maturity as celebrated in the parish is going to be measured by its "fruit" in dealing with such questions as I would now raise. Perhaps it seems strange to find ethics in a book on liturgy, but I hope the reader understands clearly the inevitable relationship between good liturgy and good living.

What is the nature of *life?* In the face of such issues as abortion, medical so-called "life-support systems," and euthanasia, when is a person alive? Your mother has had three operations for cancer, and has suffered from an organic brain disease that has left her unable to relate to time, place, or persons. She has developed pneumonia and is being assisted in breathing. Does the maturing Christian keep up the assistance? What if you and your husband come up with an unwanted pregnancy? You already have three children, and you are thirty-nine. Does the maturing Christian declare, "I own my body," and rush to get an abortion?

What about the *economy* and *poverty?* Can we rightly expend the vast majority of the earth's resources when we are only a minority of its people? We have to face the question of private property, which the encyclicals of John XXIII called a natural right. Is it? A businessman recently asked me if he as a Christian could pay "kickbacks" if he judged them necessary for the survival of his business. At least he asked the question. How does the maturing Christian answer?

What are our ideas on *progress?* Does the Church endorse, by action if not by word, the notion that salvation is tied up with being "bigger" or "more" or "higher"? Is production a Christian value, or are we more concerned with quality of being? What does it mean for the mature Christian "to have"? If we judge someone by his "fruits," does this mean what he "makes"?

Let us think about *sexuality* and the *family.* I am often asked these days whether or not I think the nuclear family will survive or whether it even ought to be saved. Not a few suggest that "secondary sexual relationships" (we used to call it adultery) are highly desirable in a free person and in so-called "open marriage." Women's liberation is a real issue, as is homosexuality. What does the maturing Christian think about this? Can he or she deal with it at more than the emotional level of the doctrinaire conservative or liberal?

As I have suggested, it may surprise the reader that these are the questions I raise in a discussion of the parish as an agency of one's coming of age in the Church. My point is that this is the "fruit" of coming of age in the Church and that this is where the parish concern should be: to make more effective by ritual celebration the point at which a Christian affirms his faith as expressed in clear values that transcend the sociocultural conditioning of our times. My fear is that this is not where the parish concern is, and because all of these issues and many more involve a risk in working them through, we avoid them. Consequently, the parish is a bore.

When the new order of Christian nurture—Baptism,

first Communion, and Confirmation—was first advanced some five years ago, I was surprised by the emotional reaction of many clergy. Now on reflection I see it was a real threat to them. They saw the Confirmation class disappearing, which was something in which they found a great deal of identity. For three, six, or even nine months, this class of preadolescents was something which gave them a sense of accomplishment whether or not this was true. At the same time, it gave a reason not to face the far more threatening issues of the society's values among adults.

Perhaps I am being grossly unfair. I do remember, however, that after World War II we complained that seven out of ten persons confirmed in the Church were lost to the Church by the time they were adults. We thought the solution to this was better Sunday Schools, never asking ourselves the obvious question: Is what we are doing in confirming persons at age twelve a good thing? I know of no serious scholar in the field of pastoral theology or Christian education today who says it is, yet the majority of parishes still do it. Why? Is it an action by which we avoid the pain of the real issues?

What we have in the proposed liturgical revision of Confirmation is a great opportunity to try something that the scholars do advocate: Christian education as, first of all, adult theological education. It is a chance to get out of the "kiddie business" and into the struggle with those who make the decisions for the future of our world. It has been asked over and over again how good church-going persons could get involved in the horror of Watergate. The answer is obvious. Church-going can occur for all kinds of reasons—some of them very sinful. It is not a matter of physical presence in Church. The question is: What is going on when people get to church? Are we developing mature Christians in our parishes by facing the values to which we believe God in Christ calls us?

It is my personal conviction that we need a divine legitimation of our actions as human beings.* We not only need it, we are going to have it one way or another. The parish priest must be someone adept in enabling that legitimation, both by the educational process of action and reflection within the life of the community and by the sensitive celebration of the critical moments in life of a person maturing in Christ. This means that he has to have the courage of his own moral convictions, which he lives out in the ritual life of the community. The priest and his parish have to be in the "transforming" business, not the "conforming" business, and know what that means for assisting persons to come of age, to be those in whom "grace wishes to reveal itself in history."

THE EPISCOPAL VISITATION

The recent history of the revision of the initiation rites in the Episcopal Church provides a brief insight into the efforts to identify the proper manner of coming of age in the Church. In *Prayer Book Studies 18*, published in 1970, what Cranmer began in collapsing chrismation back into Baptism was clearly spelled out, and the Standing Liturgical Commission said that we should no longer divide Christian initiation and attempt to justify a historical happenstance theologically. Some in the Church, particularly the bishops, were concerned that we were

* By "divine legitimation" I mean what the sociologists of knowledge, Peter Berger and Thomas Luckmann, describe as the fourth level of legitimation or that of the symbolic totality. Legitimation is that process whereby certain actions receive both motivation (it is something that ought to be done) and approval (it is okay to have done it).

excluding the average churchman from any sacramental relationship to the bishop and that we were not taking into account the need of the Christian to own his faith. *Prayer Book Studies 26*, which was published in 1973, therefore provided for the ritual associated with the visitation of a bishop over and beyond his participation in Christian initiation.

What will appear in the Draft Proposed Book of Common Prayer in 1976 is still a further revision. It is important, however—in the commendable desire of bishops to maintain a pastoral and sacramental relationship to the average churchman, and to affirm the need for the ritualization of our coming of age in the Church—that some of the gains of recent theological and liturgical reflection not be lost. The simple truth, which I trust is now self-evident, is that our prior practice has been confused theologically and unproductive pastorally.

The proposed ritual associated with the bishop's visitation beyond Baptism has been intentionally left ambiguous in some ways by the Standing Liturgical Commission. This is in light of the very sound Anglican principle: *lex orandi lex credendi*, meaning, roughly translated, that the shape of our prayer begets the shape of our theology. The Church really needs to try some new ways of doing things within the episcopate, because, without pointing the finger at anyone, there is reason to be unhappy with the prevailing style of the bishops' pastoral and sacramental functions.

The proposed rites for an episcopal visitation have been greeted by bishops in all kinds of ways.

First, there are those who plan to use whatever is finally authorized in just the way they used the Book of Common Prayer's "Order for Confirmation": as if it were the medieval rite of chrismation, or at least the laying on of hands with a Tridentine theology (*see* Chapter 2, page 43). The matter of reception and reaffirmation is something which they consider entirely apart from Confirmation, perhaps avoiding participation in reaffirmations altogether. This attitude raises some perplexing questions about the rechrismation of those already chrismated in the new baptismal liturgy, or what one is doing in the laying on of hands that was not already done at Baptism. There is also the issue of what to do when someone is baptized as an adult. Will "Confirmation" be required as in the past? If so, how can Baptism be considered as complete initiation? If not, there is a clear theological inconsistency here.

This strikes me as a "head-in-sand" approach. There lies behind it a kind of theological fundamentalism that refuses to deal with the historical, liturgical, and pastoral problems. As in most cases of intransigence, it blocks the contemporary Church's efforts to rethink its practice in the light of the present situation and more effectively to live that sacramental life to which I, personally speaking, am as deeply committed as anyone. Perhaps this sounds rather strong, but I think we need to challenge a practice which persists in exposing the "Achilles' heel" of our inherited sacramental theology.

Second, there is at least the occasional bishop who plans to ignore the existence of any rite for the laity, other than Baptism, which involves him. This attitude, of course, fixes liturgical revision at the level of *Prayer Book Studies 18*, which not a few believe was indeed the "high-water mark" of the Standing Liturgical Commission. Obviously, from what I have written here, I do not agree. It misses the whole value of ritualizing the maturing process of the Christian and plays too free with the tradition.

Third, there are those bishops who take the proposals of

Prayer Book Studies 26 and the subsequent revision with seriousness. Bishop William Frey of Colorado has related to me his experience with this. When he makes a visitation, he follows the practice of inviting, "after Confirmation," all those who desire to reaffirm their commitment to come forward and receive the laying on of hands.* He specifically seeks to avoid any sense of group coercion. The results have been most amazing, Frey reports. Sometimes as many as three hundred persons have come forward, and people have been deeply moved. It has become a ritual focal point for the uniting of the people of the diocese around their bishop.

Some reactions I have heard to this kind of thing have implied that the Episcopal Church is in danger of instituting a kind of "altar call." I think the only reply to this can be: Nothing is wrong with this as long as we do not deny our true heritage as opposed to our ideology or just sheer prejudice. It strikes me that the Protestant tradition, particularly well known in this country, of the personal, subjective sense of one's calling is combined here with the Catholic tradition of the sacramental and liturgical expression of our faith in the presence of the bishop. If this results in services lasting three hours, so what?

I for one would modify Bishop Frey's informal invitation, however, to require, as a minimum, some prior notification of the parish priest. I think that if we take the maturation process and its ritualization seriously, there needs to be a conversation and consultation about what

* In the proposed Book of Common Prayer the Standing Liturgical Commission has left the matter of the sacramental action of reception and reaffirmation ambiguous. It is the hope of the drafting committee that in all three actions—Confirmation, reception, and reaffirmation—the bishop will lay his hands upon the recipient. We did believe we had to leave room, however, for the conscience of those who could not break from the old way of thinking.

we understand ourselves to be doing. The possibility of preparation in the form of instruction and/or service seems to me to be highly commendable. There would be great value in some action and reflection prior to this kind of affirmation. It would also reinforce the relationship between the process of theological education and the liturgical life of the parish.

Certainly this new practice becomes a resource for cementing that pastoral relationship between the bishop and the laity. I get the feeling—and I cannot document this—that part of the reason some bishops may have a "zap" notion of Confirmation is because they have little time to do anything more than "zap" people. The image that comes to my mind is of "planting a seed" in a person, as on a mechanized farm, which then is watered and cultivated by the parish priest. The bishop cannot take the time to develop any personal rapport, but at least he has given this "zap" or "seed" which is his alone to give. Perhaps this is an unkind use of terms, but I do not think we want to dignify what is implied by this behavior, and such words as "zap" or "seed" convey the fact that we are faced here with bad theology. To my mind it is not without significance that if you ask the average Episcopalian, "Who confirmed you?" he is just as likely to give you the name of the presenting priest as the bishop.

It seems to me that the proposed rite for a bishop's visitation becomes a solid ritual base for a strong pastoral identification of the bishop with the people when a practice is instituted much like that which Bishop Donald Davies of Dallas proposes. Bishop Davies plans to spend eight days a year at one stretch in each of the deaneries of his diocese. I assume this will include two Sundays and the intervening week, and it will enable him to make parish calls, visit the sick, consult with persons, and be a part of the life of a number of parishes. It provides not only a context where persons can come to see him as more than an administrator, but the sacramental of the continuity of the Catholic Church, something which has been lacking since the fourth century.

In my own ministry I have discovered there is a unique power in a priestly relationship in which one is permanently involved, but not to a point of familiarity where individual foibles become an irritant. While I was at Nashotah House in Wisconsin, I had a small mission fifty miles from my home at which I was generally present only on Sundays. I believe my effectiveness and my "staying power" were enhanced by my limited presence among the members of that congregation. This was possible, of course, because they were willing at the same time to exercise a ministry among themselves. When I left after six and a half years, there was only one clergyman in this town of 8,000 who had been there longer than I, and that only by six months. I think this kind of pastoral relationship has possibilities for diocesan bishops, and the laying on of hands can be a powerful instrument in sacramentally effecting the results of that bond.

SUMMARY

My purpose in this last chapter has been to make a rough sketch of what the coming of age in the Church might be like if we accept the intention of the drafting committee on Christian Initiation of the Standing Liturgical Commission of the Episcopal Church. The proposed document is the Commission's; the sketch is mine. It is of necessity imprecise, because I would hope that time and use would not only sharpen our theology of Christian maturing, but also our accompanying liturgical practice.

In stretching our imagination I have made the following points, which build upon the conclusions of the previous three chapters.

First, the desire to affirm one's faith is part of the maturing process, where there are certain critical points in our development. I think that John Westerhoff has much to offer in giving clarity to this process, and I also believe that there is ample evidence in the life of the Church of concrete illustrations of what I mean.

Second, the parish needs to abandon its studied pursuit of triviality and become a context for the individual's faith struggle. This struggle is necessarily one in which the experience of God and the explication of values go hand in hand. I am one of those who believes that a prophet is a mystic in action and that ritual and witness are two sides of the same life.

Third, it is to be hoped that the episcopal visitation can become a significant time in the life of a parish or deanery, where the laying on of hands becomes a ritual expression of the ministry of the bishop. This will take some rethinking of the use of time, but then the Church is about fifteen hundred years overdue for that kind of consideration.

In conclusion, it should be clear that the purpose of this book has not been to advocate change for its own sake, to play down the role of the bishop in the life of the Church, or to engage in some variety of paleographical quest of the "golden age" of liturgy. The charge of all three of these possibilities has been known to pass the lips of the opposition to *Prayer Book Studies 26*, along with the rather simplistic suggestion that Confirmation has been abolished.

The issue is how to ritualize the coming of age by the grace of God of persons in the Church. The data of the tradition and the present situation, reasonably examined, show that some change—perhaps a rather traumatic change for some—is needed. Certainly it is obvious that in whatever we do the place of the bishops is essential as the pastoral and sacramental center of the Church's life, despite the emphasis upon the concrete, particular place of the local congregation.

Whereas we can turn to the past for guidance, our situation today, like every situation in history, is unique. It never has been quite the way it is now and it never will be again. We can look to the example and power of the paschal mysteries of Christ's passion, but that is to call up for our emulation the faith of our Lord. There is no "golden age." God is our future.

The question that faces the Church is, of course, one of faith. Do we really believe that the presence of God is with us now, so that we might have courage at this time to engage the present needs with an imagination informed by the eternal truth? We are as fallible now as men were four hundred, eight hundred, or twelve hundred years ago; but not necessarily any more so. The acknowledgment of our fallibility cannot absolve us from our God-given task to prepare as best we can instruments for God's graceful intervention into the lives of sinners in this present age; just as men of old gathered, prayed, and trusted that as God was known in the human flesh of Christ so shall his power be found in the cultic gestures of persons like you and me.